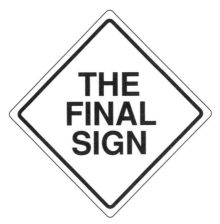

THE FINAL SIGN

Will You Know What to Look for at the End of the Age?

by

PETER YOUNGREN

ALBURY PUBLISHING
TULSA, OKLAHOMA

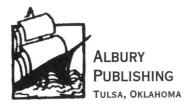

Unless otherwise indicated, all Scripture quotations are taken from the *New King James Version* of the Bible. Copyright © 1979, 1980, 1982 by Thomas Nelson, Inc., Publishers. Used by permission.

Scripture quotations marked KJV were taken from the *King James Version* of the Bible.

The Final Sign: Will You Know What to Look for at the End of the Age?
ISBN 1-57778-071-X

P. O. Box 1891
Niagara Falls, New York 14302

Published by ALBURY PUBLISHING
P. O. Box 470406
Tulsa, Oklahoma 74147-0406

Printed in the United States of America.

TABLE OF CONTENTS

Dedication......5

Acknowledgements......7

Section One: He Is Coming

1 He Is Coming...But When?......11

2 His Coming Solves Society's Problems......19

Section Two: He Is Coming at the Last Trumpet

3 The Last Trumpet......31

4 Paul Blew the Trumpet......39

5 The A.D. 49 Conference......43

6 A Vision of Fulfilled Prophecy......51

7 Council in Hell......57

8 Making Hell Tremble......69

Section Three: He Is Coming at Harvest Time

9 The Harvest......81

10 Jesus' Prophecies About the Harvest......91

11 End-Time Myths......97

12 End-Time Acceleration......115

13 The Eleventh Hour......121

14 Seven Signs of the Harvest......127

Section Four: The Final Sign

15 The Final Sign That Must Be Fulfilled......137

16 Ten Challenges Before His Coming......143

17 Bring Back the King......163

Endnotes......173

Appendix: World Statistics......177

About Peter Youngren......185

DEDICATION

To the students and alumni of World Impact Bible Institute. The vision of God's end-time plan is committed to you. In whatever field of endeavor you find yourselves — business, education, full-time ministry, or other — remember that you are called to know God, to be strong, and to do exploits. (See Daniel 11:32.) You are marked by God to fulfill the divine destiny on your lives. You are end-time harvesters.

P.Y.

ACKNOWLEDGEMENTS

Special thanks to Clara Ampofo, Fred Mast, and Grace Priest for your valuable contribution in typing, retyping, and editing this manuscript.

SECTION 1

HE IS COMING

CHAPTER 1

HE IS COMING...BUT WHEN?

JESUS PROMISED THAT HE WOULD COME BACK. It is His idea. Christians worldwide are awaiting His return. Preachers have declared His imminent return for as long as I can remember. Yet, He has not come back. Is there something wrong? When will He return?

It was July 1967, and I was at a Christian youth camp. I walked behind the boys' dormitory, perplexed with many thoughts. The conversation I had overheard between two pastors, both of whom I highly admired, had left me unsettled. Just a few weeks earlier the world had watched in disbelief as the tiny nation of Israel had taken on and defeated the surrounding Arab nations many times its size — in just six days of war.

The two preachers had been discussing this event in light of biblical prophecy and were wondering aloud whether or not Jesus would come back before the end of the youth camp. As a 12-year-old, I was worried. The camp was to last three weeks — would I see my parents before the Rapture? I felt a strong call of God on my life — but now, would I even have the opportunity to serve God?

Having been raised in an evangelical church, I was well versed in the scripture that said Jesus will come back when the Gentiles no longer trample Jerusalem underfoot: **"And Jerusalem will be trampled by Gentiles until the times of the Gentiles are fulfilled"** (Luke 21:24). Now, it seemed the Six-Day War had fulfilled this prophecy. Jerusalem was recaptured by the Jews. Had the last sign before the return of the Lord Jesus just been fulfilled?

Quietly I wished, "Oh, Lord Jesus, don't come back yet. I want to enjoy life for awhile."

Two and a half years later, New Year's Eve 1969, I attended a Watchnight Service sponsored by all the evangelical churches in the town where I lived. With a new decade about to dawn, the preacher was passionately declaring many biblical evidences of the imminent return of the Lord Jesus.

"The signs of the times indicate that this will be the last New Year's Eve service any one of us will ever attend because Jesus is coming...." I can still remember the preacher's words clearly. He then added, "If He does not come this year, there is absolutely no chance that we'll ever see another decade beyond the '70s."

Three years later, while I was attending a Bible college in the eastern United States, a well-known minister received a "vision." Copies of a cassette on which he shared what had been put into his heart were circulating on campus. It triggered the question: Will Jesus come back before the end of the school year? Many openly wondered, "Is there any sense in staying in school?"

Almost fifteen years later, the book *88 Reasons Why Jesus Is Coming Back in 1988* sold millions of copies. When 1988 passed, the author, claiming to have miscalculated by one year, wrote its sequel, *89 Reasons Why Jesus Is Coming Back in 1989.* We all know the results of that prediction.

In light of the second millennium, many are wondering, "Is *this* the year when Jesus will come back?"

In light of the second millennium, many are wondering, "Is *this* the year when Jesus will come back?" But history records that at the end of the first millennium many were expecting Christ's imminent return. Missiologist David B. Barrett writes under the chapter heading, *"Mass Hysteria In AD 1000,"*

> "In the year AD 960, Bernard of Thuringia predicted the imminent end of the world...Alarm spread throughout Europe as the end of the first millennium approached. By AD 999, multitudes were journeying to Jerusalem to await the second coming of Christ as believed to be prophesied in the Apocrypha and expected in AD

> 1000. The millennial year was preceded by widespread terrors as panic-stricken mobs thronged into Rome and Jerusalem to await the end. Richard Erdoes, in his new book, *AD 1000: Living on the Brink of Apocalypse* (1988), vividly describes the tension in St. Peter's basilica in Rome as the brilliant scientist Gerbert of Aurillac, now Pope Sylvester II, celebrated midnight mass on New Year's Eve, AD 999, regarded as the dreaded eve of the Millennium, the Final Hour, the onset of the Day of Wrath. For decades afterwards, millennial fever gripped Christendom. By the year AD 1060, vast numbers of medieval millenarian movements had arisen, involving millions of desperate rebels, radicals, and rootless poor seeking hope in a newer world."[1]

I am not suggesting that we should ignore the significance of Christ's return. On the contrary, any believer, like Paul, ought to earnestly "look for His appearing." (See Titus 2:13.) Yet, so many well-meaning Christians have made erroneous projections concerning Christ's return. In the late 1930s many respected Bible teachers taught as fact that Adolf Hitler was the Antichrist and that Benito Mussolini, Italy's fascist dictator, was the false prophet.

You may be wondering from which perspective I am writing. Am I advocating pre-tribulation, mid-tribulation, or post-tribulation Rapture? You may think I am being negative and unfair in reference to those who endeavor to discern the signs of the end times. On the contrary, I too am looking for His coming in this generation.

Any time there is a move of the Holy Spirit, there seems to be an emphasis on the return of Jesus. It is a message that the Holy Spirit wants to bring to the forefront.

There are numerous books available on end-time prophecy which deal with the timing of the Rapture in detail. This book, however, details a prophetic end-time event which is expressed throughout Scripture and yet is virtually overlooked in much end-time teaching.

It is natural for believers to passionately long for Jesus to come back. The Bible commands us to anticipate Christ's return, so I would rather err on the side of being overzealous in anticipating this wonderful event than to ignore it altogether.

Yet, as a believer, I demonstrate my true love for Christ by keeping my priorities as He desires them to be. This means the most important area is the one He told us to focus upon. I want to do what He considers important. Christ's end-time focus must be mine.

There is a tremendous fascination throughout the world concerning the future. Currently, there is a prevalent sense that things will not remain the same; everything is in a state of flux. Only a few years ago the dismantling of the Soviet Union seemed inconceivable. In the same way, it may seem unimaginable that this present age will cease and that another age will follow. Yet, that is exactly what will happen.

Unbelievers also sense that a "new age" is coming. They have talked of the "Age of Aquarius," a term popularized in the 1960s and 70s. Of course, this and other "spiritual awakenings," such as looking to a "new world order," are hell's counterfeit to God's millennial kingdom. Instead of a "new age" kingdom, the King of kings and Lord of lords is coming back to rule and reign. Yes, the dawning of a new age is upon us, but not the "new age" concept touted by the media.

Can we and *should* we know the time of the Lord's return?

Obviously, in view of Jesus' statement, **"But of that day and hour no one knows, not even the angels of heaven, but My Father only"** (Matthew 24:36), exact date-setting is out of the question. Yet at the same time, God says that He **does nothing, unless He reveals His secret to His servants the prophets** (Amos 3:7).

This indicates that at least God's people can and should know the seasons and general timings of God. After all, Simeon and Anna were both guided by the Holy Spirit and understood enough of the timings of God to come to the temple and look for the Messiah. (See Luke 2:25-38.) Though the general population of Israel was totally unaware that their Messiah had been born in Bethlehem, those who walked with

God had a sense of the destiny at hand. Similarly, in our time believers sense that Christ's return is imminent.

Is there one specific sign that tells us He is coming? If so, what is that sign? Have all the prophecies concerning His return been fulfilled?

The answer to the last question is a resounding no. There is one major world event that must yet take place. It is an unparalleled event in human history involving you and me. It is a last sign that must be fulfilled before Jesus' return, and it is very near.

By the end of this book we will have carefully analyzed this sign. It is of utmost importance that we understand God's plan for the Church. Our destiny as believers depends on it. Recently, I came across a study which revealed that 90 percent of all readers never go beyond a book's first chapter. If this were to be true for you and this book, you would miss the revelation of three significant prophecies concerning:

1. *Jesus' return at the last trumpet.* What is this last trumpet? How will we know when it has sounded?
2. *Jesus' return and the end-time harvest.* How will this affect our family and our unsaved loved ones, our city, and our church?
3. *The one sign of Jesus' coming that must yet be fulfilled.* What is this sign? How will we know that it has been fulfilled?

Your future and your purpose in life depend on a proper understanding of these truths. While God has an individual plan and purpose for you, that plan fits in with His overall plan for the world. Journey with me through this book and find out how you fit into God's end-time program.

CHAPTER 2

HIS COMING SOLVES SOCIETY'S PROBLEMS

TWO THOUSAND YEARS AGO, on the Mount of Olives in Jerusalem, Jesus' disciples wanted to know about the future. They asked Him, **What will be the sign of Your coming, and of the end of the age?** (Matthew 24:3).

Even before Jesus had departed from them, they were already looking for His return. Jesus' followers knew that the world would never be everything God intended it to be until Christ returned. According to the Old Testament prophets, Jesus' return would spell the solution to human problems.

In a moment we will look at a few of those Old Testament prophecies. However, first let's consider our current circumstances. We notice several facts:

- Evil and sin still prevail. Something is wrong on planet earth.
- Jesus has not yet raptured the Church. We are still here.
- Jesus has not yet returned to establish His kingdom.

Certainly God knows that the world is in trouble, so why doesn't Christ hurry back to straighten things out? Undoubtedly, the return of Jesus will provide the final solution to every human crisis.

The Old Testament prophet Micah foretold of a future time in history when the Messiah would rule and reign on earth in peace:

> **Now it shall come to pass in the latter days that the mountain of the Lord's house shall be established on the top of the mountains, and shall be exalted above the hills; and peoples shall flow to it.**
>
> **Many nations shall come and say, "Come, and let us go up to the mountain of the Lord, to the house of the God of Jacob; He will teach us His ways, and we shall walk in His paths." For out of Zion the law shall go forth, and the word of the Lord from Jerusalem.**
>
> **He shall judge between many peoples, and rebuke strong nations afar off; they shall beat their swords into plowshares, and their spears into pruning hooks; nation shall not lift up sword against nation, neither shall they learn war anymore.** **Micah 4:1-3**

What a world! There will be no wars. The United Nations will have no need to negotiate peace between nations because "swords" will have become "plowshares." The peace talks in the Middle East will be finished forever.

Psalm 72 is another visionary account of what life will be like when the Messiah rules the earth. UNESCO, WHO, UNICEF and other such organizations will no longer be required. For the first time since the Garden of Eden, there will be perfect peace, equality, solidarity, and justice on earth. Some of the characteristics of this peace kingdom outlined in Psalm 72 are:

- Justice for the poor (vv. 2,4)
- Care and nourishment for needy children (v. 4)
- A flourishing of righteousness and peace (v. 7)
- An end to oppression and violence (vv. 12-14)
- A cessation of famines and food shortages (v. 16).

We cannot help but exclaim, "What a wonderful world!" Why hasn't Jesus come back to establish this kind of society? The return of Jesus will finally solve human problems which politicians, relief organizations, and well-meaning individuals wrestle with daily.

Time and space do not allow this book to thoroughly cover the large amounts of scriptural references to the glorious day when God's kingdom will be established on earth. However, another brief example of this type of scripture is found in Isaiah, in which the prophet says of the Lord:

> **He shall judge between the nations, and rebuke many people; they shall beat their swords into plowshares, and their spears into pruning hooks; nation shall not lift up sword against nation, neither shall they learn war anymore.** **Isaiah 2:4**

There will be no crisis in Iraq, no civil war in Rwanda, and no violence in the inner cities. The fighting in Bosnia-Hercegovina will have ceased forever. The Middle East question will be settled. Peace will reign supreme!

In our hearts we yearn for this day and cry out, "Come quickly, Lord Jesus!"

Bible-believing Christians — people who love God — have varied views on some of the details of the book of Revelation. Yet, there is one area where we do not differ: every born-again believer longs for the return of Jesus. We look for the time when we will rule and reign together with Christ on the earth. (See Revelation 5:10.)

Paul yearned for this day. As a matter of fact, it seems he expected Jesus to come back in his own lifetime. The church of Thessalonica had become so preoccupied with the return of Jesus that they stopped their daily work to fully devote themselves to their anticipation of His coming. Others claimed that the day of the Lord had already come. This is why Paul wrote:

Now, brethren, concerning the coming of our Lord Jesus Christ and our gathering together to Him, we ask you,

not to be soon shaken in mind or troubled, either by spirit or by word or by letter, as if from us, as though the day of Christ had come. 2 Thessalonians 2:1,2

Paul corrected those who, because of a preoccupation with the Lord's return, refused to work. Instead, he exhorted the church in Thessalonica not to become **weary** in doing good while they waited for the coming of the Lord:

But as for you, brethren, do not grow weary in doing good. 2 Thessalonians 3:13

Jesus is coming back. Yet, in order for this to happen, we must not become preoccupied with setting dates for His coming or with end-time speculations. Instead, we must focus on the task of the Church, which is to ensure that every ethnic group on the earth has a witness of the Gospel of the kingdom:

"And the gospel must first be preached to all the nations." Mark 13:10

Jesus' disciples were very interested in end-time prophecy. They asked Him, **"Lord, will You at this time restore the kingdom to Israel?"** (Acts 1:6). Listen carefully to Jesus' response:

And He said to them, "It is not for you to know times or seasons which the Father has put in His own authority.

"But you shall receive power when the Holy Spirit has come upon you; and you shall be witnesses to Me in Jerusalem, and in all Judea and Samaria, and to the end of the earth." Acts 1:7-8

Notice that the disciples' focus was on *times* and *seasons*, while Jesus' focus was on the *task* He had given to them.

Notice that the disciples' focus was on *times* and *seasons*, while Jesus' focus was on the *task* He had given to them.

Just as the disciples and the church in Thessalonica had to be cautioned about excessive enthusiasm concerning end-time prophecy, caution may be in order today. The Church must become focused on fulfilling Matthew 24:14:

"And this gospel of the kingdom will be preached in all the world as a witness to all the nations, and then the end will come."

The word **nations**, as translated in the *New King James* text, is the Greek word *ethnos.*[1] Its Greek definition more clearly denotes tribe or ethnic group, rather than whole nations: An ethnic group is any group of people originating

The gospel of the kingdom, therefore, means more than just a Gospel tract or a Christian shortwave radio signal....

from or distinguished by race, language, and/or culture.[2] To substantiate this, there are only 260 nations in the world, but more than 20,000 ethnic groups.

The term, **gospel of the kingdom,** implies much more than we might think at first glance. A kingdom is a domain or area in which a king exercises authority. The kingdom of God today is the rule and power of Christ being exercised in and through a people living in a particular area. The **gospel of the kingdom,** therefore, means more than just a Gospel tract or a Christian shortwave radio signal going into a particular area. It means that there must be a **witness** to the rule and power of Christ being demonstrated. While it does not mean that everyone in every ethnic group will be saved, neither does it mean that a few radio programs or leaflets produced in a certain language indicate that the people who speak that language have been reached.

A case in point is Saudi Arabia. It is not enough that there are foreign workers in Saudi Arabia who believe in Christ, even though those foreign workers are allowed a measure of freedom to worship. Rather, there must be a demonstration of the rule and authority of Jesus Christ and His Church demonstrated to and within the Saudi population.

A "witness" is a person who gives evidence in a court session. The court will not accept hearsay, but only the word of an individual who can testify of what he or she has personally seen or heard. A "witness" of the Gospel of the kingdom of God consists of real-life, flesh-and-blood testimonies of the transforming power of Christ within every culture.

Both the universal Church and the local church have been given the authority to overcome the gates of hell. (See Matthew 16:18 KJV.) Yet it is the presence of the local church among all ethnic groups that becomes a witness of the Gospel of God's kingdom at a grass-roots level.

By now you may feel somewhat discouraged as you think of the enormity of the task Christ has given to us believers. How can we ever complete such a monumental task? Frankly, it does seem impossible, except for an often overlooked prophecy of which Jesus spoke concerning the end time. The fulfillment of that prophecy will revolutionize our thinking concerning not only our friends and loved ones, but about *how* hundreds of millions will be swept into God's kingdom.

Our zeal ought to be focused, not so much on world events and speculation as to how they fit in with Bible prophecy, but instead, on bringing in the harvest of the earth in our lifetime. We can see Jesus Christ come back. Matthew 24:14 can be fulfilled. Get ready in the next few chapters as we dig deep into these prophecies that will profoundly affect your life.

> **He who testifies to these things says, "Surely I am coming quickly." Amen. Even so, come, Lord Jesus!**
>
> **Revelation 22:20**

SECTION 2

HE IS COMING AT THE LAST TRUMPET

CHAPTER 3

THE LAST TRUMPET

THE EARLY MORNING AIR WAS PIERCED by the sound of a trumpet. The people of Jerusalem stirred out of their slumber. Two men looked at each other and broke into peals of laughter. They had been awake most of the night, anticipating what this morning would bring — the solo strains of the trumpet signaling the Year of Jubilee.

Fifteen years earlier, their father had lost some prized real estate holdings through bad business dealings. This valuable property had been in the family for generations. Before his death, their father had reminded them, "When the Year of Jubilee comes, your debts will be canceled; possessions will be returned to their rightful owner. As soon as you hear the trumpet sound, go and repossess your inheritance."

After hearing the welcome sound of the trumpet, the young men took only seconds to dash out of the simple servants' quarters. For the last few years they had been working for a landowner, trying to pay off the family debt with their meagre earnings.

With great confidence, they hurried to the house of the landowner who had taken over their family's property and demanded their rightful ownership. The Year of Jubilee had come.

Across town, in another of Jerusalem's low-income sections, a whole family had been awake several hours before dawn, eagerly anticipating the moment when the trumpet would sound. Forty-five years earlier, shortly after the last Year of Jubilee, their grandparents had lost the family estate through a bad investment. For almost two generations they had worked at menial labor, all the while knowing that another Year of Jubilee would come. Then they would be free from all debts and, once again, possess their former estate. When the resonating sound of the shofar broke the morning air, they dashed out the door of their humble home to take possession of what had been lost to them for so long.

Nearby, a mother was literally jumping with joy. Her financial difficulty had forced her to sell her sons as bondsmen. For seven years they had worked to pay off the family debt. Although they had been treated as slaves, their spirits had remained high because they knew the Year of Jubilee was coming. All captives would be set free and all debts canceled.

When the trumpet sound announced the Year of Jubilee, the mother rushed out the door to see her sons run toward her house. A new life was about to begin for this family.

◆ ◆ ◆

The books of Moses speak at length about the Year of Jubilee and the freedom it brought to the people:

> **"'And you shall consecrate the fiftieth year, and proclaim liberty throughout all the land to all its inhabitants. It shall be a Jubilee for you; and each of you shall return to his possession, and each of you shall return to his family.'" Leviticus 25:10**

Is there a connection between...the Year of Jubilee trumpet and the fact that Jesus is coming back "at the last trumpet"?

Is there a connection between the sounding of the Old Testament, Year of Jubilee trumpet and the fact that Jesus is coming back "at the last trumpet"?

Paul declared that the trumpet of God would announce Jesus' return:

> **For the Lord Himself will descend from heaven with a shout, with the voice of an archangel, and with the trumpet of God. And the dead in Christ will rise first.**
>
> **Then we who are alive and remain shall be caught up together with them in the clouds to meet the Lord in the air. And thus we shall always be with the Lord.**
>
> **1 Thessalonians 4:16,17**

Paul further clarified what this trumpet signifies, by calling it the last trumpet:

> **Behold, I tell you a mystery: We shall not all sleep, but we shall all be changed —**
>
> **in a moment, in the twinkling of an eye, at the last trumpet. For the trumpet will sound, and the dead will be raised incorruptible, and we shall be changed.**
>
> **1 Corinthians 15:51,52**

If you closely study the letters of Paul, a Hebrew scholar, you will find that he often refers to the Hebrew faith and custom. In the two preceding Scripture passages he is undoubtedly referring to trumpets as they were used in the religious celebrations of the nation of Israel.

Notice how the trumpet or *shofar* (ram's horn) was used to declare the Year of Jubilee:

> **"'And you shall count seven sabbaths of years for yourself, seven times seven years; and the time of the seven sabbaths of years shall be to you forty-nine years.**
>
> **'Then you shall cause the trumpet of the Jubilee to sound on the tenth day of the seventh month; on the**

> **The spreading of the Levites throughout the land facilitated the relaying of the trumpet sound throughout Israel.**

Day of Atonement *you shall make the trumpet to sound throughout all your land.*

'And you shall consecrate the fiftieth year, and *proclaim liberty throughout all the land to all its inhabitants.* It shall be a Jubilee for you; and each of you shall return to his possession, and each of you shall return to his family.'" Leviticus 25:8-10 (emphasis added)

Note God's command: **"You shall make the trumpet to sound throughout all your land....and proclaim liberty throughout all the land to all its inhabitants."** Not everyone in Israel was able to hear the trumpet sound from Jerusalem. The priest blew the trumpet at the temple site there, but many of Israel's tribes lived far away. The tribe of Levi had not received their own land as the other tribes. Instead, they were scattered throughout all the tribes of Israel, where 48 territories had been assigned to them. (See Numbers 35:7.) While the Bible does not directly state how the trumpet sound was carried throughout all the land, it seems logical that the spreading of the Levites throughout the land facilitated the relaying of the trumpet sound throughout Israel.

In territory after territory, hour after hour, the trumpet sounded, each time announcing the Year of Jubilee to yet another region. Each time it was heard, there was rejoicing as debts were canceled and captives set free. Farther and farther the news carried into the remotest regions.

The Year of Jubilee was not fully inaugurated until the *last* region of Israel had heard the trumpet sound. The last trumpet indicated that the most remote region in the land had heard the good news of the Year of Jubilee.

Now, let's look at the connection between the year of Jubilee and the preaching of the Gospel. Jesus inaugurated His earthly ministry in the synagogue at Jerusalem by reading the words of Isaiah:

> **"The Spirit of the Lord is upon Me, because He has anointed Me to preach the gospel to the poor; He has sent Me to heal the brokenhearted, To proclaim liberty to the captives and recovery of sight to the blind, to set at liberty those who are oppressed;**
>
> **To proclaim the acceptable year of the Lord."**
>
> **Luke 4:18,19**

Jesus closed the book and told those gathered: **"Today this Scripture is fulfilled in your hearing"** (v. 21). The **acceptable year of the Lord** is the Year of Jubilee. The Year of Jubilee is a type of Jesus' work at Calvary's cross, which frees us, and cancels our debt of sin.

Nazareth was the first town to hear the sound of the New Testament Year of Jubilee. Jesus Himself proclaimed that what the people had longed for was now fulfilled. Since that inaugural moment, the news has gone forth and will continue to resound until the last region of the earth has heard the Gospel:

> **"And this gospel of the kingdom will be preached in all the world as a witness to all the nations, and then the end will come."** **Matthew 24:14**

Jesus is coming back at the sound of the last trumpet. He is coming back when every person on earth has heard the Gospel of what Jesus did for mankind at Calvary almost 2,000 years ago.

What is the last trumpet? It is the proclamation of the Gospel of the kingdom to even the remotest region of the earth. Only then can King Jesus return.

CHAPTER 4

PAUL BLEW THE TRUMPET

NO ONE WAS MORE DEDICATED TO PROCLAIMING the Gospel than the apostle Paul. He lived his life as though the propagation of the Gospel depended on him alone, while at the same time recognizing that God was using many to accomplish His purpose. So great was Paul's dedication that he also worked at a secular job to support himself and others whom he sent out to preach:

> **"I have coveted no one's silver or gold or apparel.**
>
> **"Yes, you yourselves know that these hands have provided for my necessities, and for those who were with me." Acts 20:33,34**

Paul's dedication to the Gospel is evident as he told the Romans of the passion burning in his soul:

> **I am a debtor both to Greeks and to barbarians, both to wise and to unwise.**
>
> **So, as much as is in me, I am ready to preach the gospel to you who are in Rome also.**

For I am not ashamed of the gospel of Christ, for it is the power of God to salvation for everyone who believes, for the Jew first and also for the Greek.

Romans 1:14-16

The apostle Paul was inner-driven, impelled to go into new regions to announce the Year of Jubilee and declare that the power of sin, sickness, guilt, and shame was broken. His passion was to preach to everyone on earth regardless of nationality or culture:

For there is no distinction between Jew and Greek, for the same Lord over all is rich to all who call upon Him.

For "whoever calls upon the name of the Lord shall be saved."

How then shall they call on Him in whom they have not believed? And how shall they believe in Him of whom they have not heard? And how shall they hear without a preacher?

And how shall they preach unless they are sent? As it is written: "How beautiful are the feet of those who

Paul's passion was that those *"to whom He was not announced, they shall see; and those who have not heard shall understand."*

preach the gospel of peace, who bring glad tidings of good things!" **Romans 10:12-15**

In his teaching in Romans, chapter 15, Paul frequently quoted the Old Testament to prove that God's plan of salvation included the Gentile world. Paul wrote of his drive to preach **not where Christ was named, lest I should build on another man's foundation** (Romans 15:20). Paul's passion was that those **"to whom He was not announced, they shall see; and those who have not heard shall understand"** (Romans 15:21).

Paul's enormous desire to reach the unreached hindered him from visiting Rome. He wrote to explain to the Roman believers that, since he had planned a missionary journey to Spain, he had decided to make a brief stop in Rome on the way:

> **For this reason I also have been much hindered from coming to you.**
>
> **But now no longer having a place in these parts, and having a great desire these many years to come to you,**
>
> **whenever I journey to Spain, I shall come to you. For I hope to see you on my journey, and to be helped on my way there by you, if first I may enjoy your company for a while.** **Romans 15:22-24**

An extended stay in Rome would have been a good career move for Paul.

This passage speaks volumes about Paul's attitude. An extended stay in Rome would have been a good career move for Paul, as Rome was the financial, political, and cultural center of the ancient world. He could have made some powerful and important connections there. Moreover, it seems that the church in Rome had been inviting Paul to come for some time.

Why would he refuse such a career-enhancing invitation? Of course, we know the answer. Paul was not a career preacher. He was devoted to those who had not heard the Gospel. He was working toward one goal: to bring in **the fullness of the Gentiles** (Romans 11:25).

Paul's greatest passion was to see the return of Jesus Christ, but he knew this would never happen until everyone had heard the Gospel. Nothing was more important to him than for every region to hear the Good News.

CHAPTER 5

THE A.D. 49 CONFERENCE

IN THE YEAR A.D. 49, JERUSALEM was the site of Church history's very first missions conference. Some of the Hebrew believers were having difficulty accepting Paul's Gospel theology. They believed that salvation should be obtained through a combination of faith in Christ and adherence to Judaism. Peter entered the heated discussion by affirming that an outpouring of the Holy Spirit with mighty miracles had occurred among the Gentiles. Paul and Barnabas then also declared **how many miracles and wonders God had worked through them among the Gentiles** (Acts 15:12).

James then delivered the conference's final address in which he summarized God's plan for the Church by preaching from the prophet Amos. In his sermon he gave a chronology of Church history:

> **And after they had become silent, James answered, saying, "Men and brethren, listen to me:**
>
> **"Simon has declared how God at the first visited the Gentiles to take out of them a people for His name.**

> **"And with this the words of the prophets agree, just as it is written:**
>
> **"'After this I will return and will rebuild the tabernacle of David, which has fallen down; I will rebuild its ruins, and I will set it up; so that the rest of mankind may seek the Lord, even all the Gentiles who are called by My name, says the Lord who does all these things.'" Acts 15:13-17**

Four end-time phases in Church history can be clearly distinguished from James' sermon.

END-TIME PHASE ONE:

God is visiting the Gentiles **to take out of them a people for His name** (v. 14). The Old Testament prophets and the teachings of the apostle Paul in the New Testament all confirm this truth. It is a time commonly known as "the Church Age" or "the Age of Grace." We know that we currently are living in this age by the fact that Jesus Christ has not yet returned.

Obviously, God is still "visiting the Gentiles," and the priority is to bring in **the fullness of the Gentiles** (Romans 11:25). Until this first item on God's agenda is accomplished, other prophetic events cannot happen.

END-TIME PHASE TWO:

"'After this I will return....'" **Acts 15:16**

Yes, Jesus will return. Notice His return occurs after the task of reaching the Gentiles is completed.

END-TIME PHASE THREE:

Following this event the ruined tabernacle of David will be rebuilt. This restoration is a clear reference to the salvation of the nation of Israel. Throughout history only a few Jewish people have come to faith in Christ as their Messiah. In the last few decades there has been an acceleration in Messianic Jewry, yet there is still only a minority of Jews who confess the name of Jesus.

Paul teaches in Romans, chapter 11, about the day when all of Israel shall be saved. Zechariah is just one of many who prophesied of the glorious day when natural Israel, looking to Jesus as their Messiah, will be saved:

"In that day a fountain shall be opened for the house of David and for the inhabitants of Jerusalem, for sin and for uncleanness." **Zechariah 13:1**

More about God's end-time plan for the physical Israel will be discussed in Chapter 11.

END-TIME PHASE FOUR:

> **"'So that the rest of mankind may seek the Lord....'"**
> **Acts 15:17**

This period of time is what we commonly refer to as the Millennium. Satan will be bound for 1,000 years. (See Revelation 20:2.) Jesus Christ will rule and reign with the saints of God on earth. It will be a kingdom of peace.

A survey of these four phases will tell us we are still in Phase One. Many eagerly look ahead to the fulfillment of Phase Two, Three, or even Four. Signs of these phases are eagerly discussed and analyzed. But until we finish the task of world evangelization — Phase One — we will not see Jesus return.

So why has Jesus not yet come back? Why have we not yet come to the point that fulfills the prophecy, **I will return**?

The answer is simple.

We cannot get to Phase Two until Phase One is completed. The task of bringing in the Gentiles is not yet complete. The last trumpet has not yet sounded. The remotest regions on planet earth have not yet had a witness of the kingdom of God established in them.

It doesn't matter how much "end-time prophecy" teachers try to tell us about how Jesus could come back any moment. The fact is, the Bible is abundantly clear that He will not come until the Gospel has been preached to all nations.

Yes, there is coming a United Europe...as foretold in the prophetic words of Daniel and John the Revelator. Yes, there will be a "666" mark of the beast. But neither one of these...is the sign of the end.

Some Bible teachers like to scrutinize every significant world event and speculate about its significance in relationship to Bible prophecy. Every time there is an announcement about the development of a United Europe or a technology that will facilitate the "666" imprint on a person's forehead or hand, they go to great "analytical" lengths. Many Christians buy video tapes and books dealing with such subjects.

Yes, there is coming a United Europe or, more precisely, a restored Roman Empire, as foretold in the prophetic words of Daniel and John the Revelator. Yes, there will be a "666" mark of the beast. But neither one of these, nor a host of any other details in the end-time prophecy of Scripture, is the sign of the end. It is imperative that we focus, not on speculations, but on fulfilling the one thing that must happen before Jesus returns: the *completed* task of preaching the Gospel to the Gentiles.

In the second sermon of the apostle Peter recorded in the book of Acts, Peter addressed the same subject when he said,

"And that He may send Jesus Christ, who was preached to you before,

whom heaven must receive until the times of restoration of all things, which God has spoken by the mouth of all His holy prophets since the world began."

Acts 3:20,21

The phrase, **whom heaven must receive,** could also read "whom heaven must retain."[1] Jesus will be retained in heaven until a specific time. All the things that must precede His return must be fulfilled. There are no shortcuts. In his sermon, Simon Peter then continued to explain the things that must be fulfilled:

"For Moses truly said to the fathers, 'The Lord your God will raise up for you a Prophet like me from your brethren. Him you shall hear in all things, whatever He says to you.'" **Acts 3:22**

This verse refers to the first coming of Jesus, for it is Jesus Who is the **Prophet** like Moses. Obviously, this prophecy has already been fulfilled.

Simon Peter then referred to a second prophecy:

"'And it shall be that every soul who will not hear that Prophet shall be utterly destroyed from among the people.'" **Acts 3:23**

At the time of Peter's sermon, this prophecy had not yet been fulfilled. It is clear that in A.D. 70, when the Roman conqueror Titus destroyed Jerusalem, verse 23 of Acts, chapter 3, was indeed fulfilled. Many of those who were killed, some even by crucifixion, were the very ones who had refused to believe in Jesus as their Messiah.

Then Simon Peter went on to quote a third prophecy, this one from God to Abraham:

> **"You are sons of the prophets, and of the covenant which God made with our fathers, saying to Abraham, 'And in your seed all the families of the earth shall be blessed.'"** **Acts 3:25**

Here, again, we have the unmistakable prophetic word concerning the evangelization of the world. Through Abraham's seed, **all the families of the earth shall be blessed.** Jesus must be kept in heaven until all the families of the earth are blessed with the message of His first coming. While we anxiously await His second coming, we must busy ourselves by ensuring that every ethnic group — every family of the earth — will hear the news of the Gospel.

What the prophets spoke must be fulfilled. The Gospel must reach everyone.

CHAPTER 6

A VISION OF FULFILLED PROPHECY

IT IS A.D. 96. JOHN, THE ELDERLY AND ONLY remaining of the twelve apostles of the Lamb, is exiled on the isle of Patmos. The destruction of Jerusalem, prophesied by Jesus in Matthew, chapter 24, was fulfilled 26 years ago.

John has given his life to "blow the trumpet," to announce the Year of Jubilee, to preach the Gospel. On this particular Lord's day, he is caught away in the Spirit; he sees a vision.

Suddenly, before his eyes there is an enormous crowd of people singing, ***"Salvation belongs to our God who sits on the throne, and to the Lamb!"*** *(Revelation 7:10).*

These multitudes have washed their robes and made them white in the blood of the Lamb; they are worshiping God with all their might:

> **After these things I looked, and behold, a great multitude which no one could number, of all nations, tribes, peoples, and tongues, standing before the throne and before the Lamb, clothed with white robes, with palm branches in their hands.** **Revelation 7:9**

John's heart leaps with joy as he records this vision. As a very young man, John had been present at the Mount of Olives when the disciples admired the temple buildings. Later, he shared their incredulity upon hearing Jesus say that not one stone of these beautiful buildings would be left upon another. (See Matthew 24:2.)

John had also heard Jesus prophesy about the one sign that must be fulfilled before His coming, ***"And this gospel of the kingdom will be preached in all the world as a witness to all the nations, and then the end will come"*** *(Matthew 24:14). The task had seemed overwhelming. The years he and the others had spent preaching the Gospel passed quickly. He remembers so vividly A.D. 70, when the news reached him that the Roman conqueror Titus had levelled Jerusalem and the temple to the ground. Not one stone was left upon another. Indeed, Jesus' prophetic words had been fulfilled in detail.*

Yet, in the same prophecy Jesus had said that the Gospel would be preached to all ethnicities as a witness. John had wondered at the time how this great task would be accomplished. But now, right before his eyes, he is seeing a vision depicting the very thing Jesus said would happen.

When John sees the innumerable multitude in the vision, he exclaims, "Glory to God! The task is going to be finished. The last region on planet earth will hear the Gospel. The Church will do what Jesus told us to do. Every kindred, tongue, and nation shall hear the Gospel." John has seen some large gatherings, but he is awestruck as he views this seemingly endless multitude ***which no one could number.***

The early disciples sacrificed everything for the proclamation of the Good News. They gave their lives for the cause of sounding the Gospel trumpet everywhere. The Church of Jesus Christ must continue with this same fervor today.

More than anything, hell fears believers who are committed to fulfilling the Great Commission. Christian activities — however noble and good — which have no influence on the lost and, particularly, the unreached, will not threaten hell.

Christian activities — however noble and good — which have no influence on the lost and, particularly, the unreached, will not threaten hell.

There are many things we do in the name of Jesus and for Jesus which He has not specifically asked us to do. We must be certain we are involved in those things He directs us to, such as building programs, the purchase of a new church organ, or the establishment of a Christian camp. These are all noble and worthy causes if they are Spirit-led. We need buildings, equipment, and activities in order to fulfill the Great Commission!

That reward will not be based on the things He did not ask us to do, but on the things He has asked us to do.

When we, as believers, meet Christ before His judgment seat to receive our reward, that reward will not be based on the things He did not ask us to do, but on the things He has asked us to do. Jesus very specifically asked us to take the Gospel into all the world. This will undoubtedly be very important in relationship to each person's reward. Let's see to it that our work is not **burned**, as the Bible clearly states will be the case with some:

> **For no other foundation can anyone lay than that which is laid, which is Jesus Christ.**
>
> **Now if anyone builds on this foundation with gold, silver, precious stones, wood, hay, straw,**
>
> **each one's work will become clear; for the Day will declare it, because it will be revealed by fire; and the fire will test each one's work, of what sort it is.**
>
> **If anyone's work which he has built on it endures, he will receive a reward.**
>
> **If anyone's work is burned, he will suffer loss; but he himself will be saved, yet so as through fire.**
>
> **1 Corinthians 3:11-15**

After a day's work, I return to my house and, to my amazement, I find the plumber mowing my lawn.

Imagine the following scenario. Suppose I have problems with the plumbing in my house, so I call a plumber to take care of the situation. When he arrives at my house in the morning, I give him the keys, and he assures me that everything will be taken care of by evening. After a day's work, I return to my house and, to my amazement, I find the plumber mowing my lawn. I also notice that he has put a fresh coat of paint on my porch. Immediately I begin to thank him for the "extra" work he has done.

However, before I hand over the check as payment for his labor, I inquire about the plumbing, to which he answers that he has not had a chance to look at it yet. He says, "The grass obviously needed to be cut, and your porch needed a fresh coat of paint, so I decided to do that before the plumbing." Naturally, I am not too pleased. Even though the plumber has done good things, he has not done what I specifically asked him to do.

We can do many good things in the name of the Lord, but we must not neglect to do what Jesus specifically asked us to do in His final command. Evangelism is not just for those who feel "called"; it is every believer's duty. We must find ourselves laboring in at least two of the following three areas of the Great Commission:

PRAYING:

We must pray for those who go and pray for them as they labor:

> **Then He said to them, "The harvest truly is great, but the laborers are few; therefore pray the Lord of the harvest to send out laborers into His harvest."**
>
> **Luke 10:2**

SENDING:

We must send others to preach to those who have never heard. The sending involves financial giving and personal care for those who go:

> **And how shall they preach unless they are sent?**
>
> **Romans 10:15**

GOING:

We must be involved in going ourselves:

> **For "whoever calls upon the name of the Lord shall be saved." How then shall they call on Him in whom they have not believed? And how shall they believe in Him of whom they have not heard? And how shall they hear without a preacher? Romans 10:13,14**

CHAPTER 7

COUNCIL IN HELL

IT IS APPROXIMATELY A.D. 1900.

"Well, any news?" asks Satan, looking up with an inquiring expression on his face.

"I've got great news, the very best!" responds the Prince of Northern Russia, who has just entered.

"Have any of the Inuit heard yet?" questions the eager leader, his eyes fastened on the fallen angel.

"Not one!" answers the Prince, bowing low. "No indeed, not a single individual. I have seen to that," he continues, as though gloating over a recent victory.

"Any attempts?" asks his lord in a tone of authority. "Have any attempted to get in?"

"That they have, but their efforts were foiled before they learned a word of the language!" replies the Prince, a note of triumph in his voice.

"How did it happen?" Satan is all ears now.

"Why," begins the Prince, "I was roaming back and forth within my domains, having penetrated far beyond the Arctic Circle in order to visit one of the most isolated tribes. Suddenly I was amazed to hear of two missionaries on their way from across the water. They had landed with their dog

sleds and were already well into the heart of my kingdom, Northern Russia, heading for a large tribe of Inuit."

"Yes, and what did you do?" Satan breaks in, impatient to hear the climax.

"First of all, I gathered together the hosts of darkness under my command and held a council. Many suggestions were made. Finally it was agreed that the easiest way was to freeze them to death.

"Finding that they were leaving that day for the distant tribe, and that it would in all probability take them a full month to cross the frozen ice fields that intervened, we at once began operations.

"With hearts burdened to make the Message known, they started. Confidently they 'mushed' along, but after about a week's travel, suddenly one day their food sled ran over thin ice, which broke beneath its weight, and it was immediately lost. Weary and tired, they bravely plodded on only to realize that they were in a helpless condition and still more than three weeks from their destination. They were new to the great Northland and were no match for it.

"Finally, when they were out of food, tired, weary in body, and almost ready to give up, I gave the word of command, and in a short time the wind began to blow up a storm. The snow came down in a blinding blizzard, and before morning, thanks to the fact that you, O my lord, are the Prince of the Powers of the Air, they froze to death."

"Excellent! Splendid! You have served me well," comments the fallen cherub, with a gratified expression on his once beautiful countenance.

"And what do you have to report?" he continues, turning to the Prince of Tibet, who has listened with evident satisfaction to the conversation.

"I too have a story that will fill your majesty with delight."

"Ha! Has an attempt been made to invade your kingdom as well, my Prince?" inquires Satan with a growing interest.

"That there has!" responds the Prince.

"How? Tell me about it," commands Satan, instantly on the alert.

"I was attending to my duties in the heart of Tibet when news reached me of a church that was sending out missionaries to get the Gospel into my kingdom. Naturally, I was at once on the alert, my lord. I called my forces together to discuss the whole situation, and we soon agreed on a plan that promised success.

"With great determination, two men sent out by the church traveled across China and boldly passed over the border to enter the Forbidden Land. We allowed them to advance about a three-days' journey, and then, just as it was growing dark, two savage dogs, such as are found all over the country, sprang upon them. Most desperately they fought for their lives, but finally one was dragged down and

killed. The other somehow managed to escape. We are very fortunate, however. Though these missionaries loved their Lord greatly, we have managed to keep the whole Church totally ignorant about their authority in Christ. They have been ignorant about how their Lord heals, delivers, and protects them. They don't know about the gifts of the Spirit either. This is how we have managed to destroy the lives of many missionaries."

"Yes, it is wonderful we have been able to keep them in ignorance," muses Satan. "However, you said that one escaped," the devil's musing turns to anger. "Did he get the Message to them?"

"No, my lord," responds the Prince of Tibet in assuring tones. "He had no chance. Before he could learn a word of the language, our hosts of demonic forces set him up. We stirred the people against him so he was quickly tried and sentenced. It was a scene that would have filled your majesty with delight. They sewed him up in a wet yak sling and put him out in the sun to bake. For three days he remained there, his bones slowly cracking as the skin shrank, until finally life ceased."

The room had been quickly filling as the Prince of Tibet was speaking, and, at the conclusion of his report, a great cheer rises from the entire assembly, while all bow to the majestic figure of Satan.

But a moment later, the cheering subsides, hushed by a wave of Satan's hand.

"And what do you have to report?" he asks, turning to another fallen angel. "Are you still Master of Afghanistan, my Prince?"

"That I am, your majesty," replies the one addressed, "though were it not for my faithful follower, I doubt if it would be so."

"Has an attempt been made on your domains also?" exclaims Satan in a loud voice.

"Yes, my lord, but listen and I will fill you in on all the details. We watched their advance; there were four of them — all zealous to make Him known. As you know, my lord, just inside the border of my kingdom there is a sign that meets every traveler:

ENTRANCE FORBIDDEN

"The missionaries knelt down around the sign and prayed, but, in spite of this, our forces prevailed. Fifty feet from the sign, on a pile of rocks, sat an Afghan guard, rifle in hand. After praying, the little company stepped boldly over the border and entered the Forbidden Land. The guard allowed them to advance 20 paces, then, like a flash of lightning, three shots were fired, and three of the company lay on the ground, two of them dead, the third wounded. A friend dragged the wounded man back to the border, where, after

a short sickness, he died. Then he himself lost heart and fled from the country."

Satan finally turned to the ruler of the Unreached Lands. "How are things in the other lands?" he asks. "Are we keeping the Gospel Army from any ethnic group?"

"The Church is still kept ignorant in many places. There are nations and tribes that the Church hasn't even tried to reach. In India alone there are hundreds of millions who have never once heard the Gospel. Our forces are hard at work to keep the Church more concerned with financing projects for their own enjoyment than they are with sending missionaries to places where no one has gone. The Church has been asleep when it comes to these places," replies the ruler.

"Excellent!" responds the devil.

Prolonged cheering follows this speech. Satan is more ecstatic than anyone, for he is still in possession of many unreached lands. The Message and the Name have been kept out.

"Tell us, O mighty one, why is it so important that these people not hear the Message? Don't you know that many have heard the Message and that it is available in many parts of the world?"

"Yes, I know these things. Listen, and I will explain why I am so jealous and protective of the unreached areas of the earth," answers Satan, and all draw near to hear.

"There are several prophecies, perhaps best summed up in the one which reads, ***This gospel of the kingdom shall be preached in all the world for a witness unto all nations; and then shall the end come*** *(Matthew 24:14 KJV).*

"Many Christians are so naive. They live in a fantasy world. They believe all these so-called prophecies about how He shall come back on such and such a date. It is very funny, since the Bible says no one knows the date," laughs Satan.

"In addition, He can't come back until every tribe, nation, and tongue have heard the message. When they all have heard, when what they call the Great Commission has been fulfilled, then that will be the sign that the end has come.

"It even says, ***I beheld...a great multitude, which no man could number, of all nations, and kindreds, and people, and tongues*** *(Revelation 7:9 KJV). So the most important thing is not how many missionaries are sent to countries that are already evangelized...we must keep them from the unreached areas."*

"Then," breaks in the Prince of Nepal, "if we can keep every messenger out of the Unreached Lands, we can prevent His coming to reign on the earth and so frustrate the purposes of the Most High."

As the great plan dawns upon them, they shout with derision and hurry back to their empires, more determined than ever to prevent the escape of a single soul.

◆ ◆ ◆

Many years have passed. Restlessly, His Satanic Majesty paces back and forth. Dark frowns overshadow his countenance. It is apparent that something of an unusual nature is troubling him.

"It must not be!" he mutters to himself. "And the very plan, too," he continues in a louder tone. "Yes, the very plan. They seem to have caught a vision of it at last. 'Evangelize,' 'Pioneer,' I don't like those words! I detest their purpose, their object to hasten the return of the Lord by preaching the Gospel ***in all the world for a witness unto all nations*** *(Matthew 24:14 KJV). They must not* ***go...into all the world, and preach the gospel to every creature*** *(Mark 16:15 KJV).*

"We must stop these zealots whose primary aim is to engage in only such activities as contribute to world evangelism. These are the ones who change our purpose, these who want to preach wherever His name has not been heard.

"And that dreadful phrase of theirs: 'Bring back the King.' It shall not be! I must frustrate their purposes! The King! What will happen to me when He comes? I must call a council immediately."

In a few minutes they are all present. All the principalities and powers and rulers of darkness are gathered. Satan starts to speak: "Prince of Northern Russia, step forward!"

Trembling and afraid, he approaches his lord.

"Prince of Northern Russia, have they entered yet?"

"Yes, my lord, they have," he slowly responds.

"How?" thunders Satan, hardly able to control himself. "Why didn't you guard my empire better?"

"We did our best, your majesty, but to no avail. The frozen bodies of the first two were discovered. Then we kept the others ignorant for many years through atheistic communism. It did not make their church quit. It only made them more determined to get the Gospel to Northern Russia. They have been sending missionaries. We stopped some, but finally they broke through. They were guarded and protected by angels; we could no longer drive them out. Today, there are tens of thousands of Inuit in the kingdom of God."

Satan fumes and bellows out his rage. The very air fills with his anger. He continues: "Prince of Tibet, stand forth! You have a better report to give, I hope!"

"No, my lord."

"What! Have any heard the Name in your domain?"

"I couldn't prevent it. We did our best. There has been a revival movement in the Church. People are dedicating themselves, their finances, and their prayers for the purpose of taking the Gospel to everyone. We tried to destroy them with starvation, disease, and many other pitfalls. We pitted political and religious leaders against them, but nothing has been able to stop them. These believers know their authority in the Name. Now there are scores of Tibetans who have

been taken out of our grip, and many others who have heard the Message."

With a rage beyond words, Satan turns finally to the Prince of Afghanistan, saying, "Step forward!"

There is a moment of hesitation, then, with slow steps and downcast eyes, he stands forth.

"Prince of Afghanistan, you have always guarded your domain well. I take it you have not failed me."

There is no reply.

"Speak! Have they entered?"

"Yes, they have. We tried everything to stop them, but there was no use. The whole Church was praying for the missionaries in my domain. Their prayers lifted up and protected the missionaries, so we were powerless. Angels constantly guarded them. People are now starting to get saved, only a few dozen, but there are some."

Finally, Satan turns to the ruler of the Unreached Lands. "Is your domain still untouched by the Gospel?"

"No, I am afraid not," replies the ruler of the Unreached Lands. "I have been trying to hold on to my domain, but the Church has awakened, and there is a mighty force of people being raised up. The Gospel is now beginning to touch every area of my domain.

"This new generation knows their God, and they are doing great exploits. They know that their Lord heals, delivers, and protects them, as well as miraculously saves them.

They know their authority in their Lord. We can't handle them. Remember that their Lord promised there would be a great harvest at the end of the age. It seems that great harvest is upon us."

"And now," roars Satan, "do what you can before all is lost. Every area is being invaded by these people. The sign of His coming must not be fulfilled, the end of the age must not come."[1]

CHAPTER 8

MAKING HELL TREMBLE

THIS CAN BE THE GENERATION THAT BLOWS the last trumpet, the generation that defeats Satan's purposes and welcomes King Jesus back to earth.

We are living in a spiritual combat zone. The forces of hell are doing everything in their power to hold back the coming of the Lord. However, there is hope. There is a breed of believers who are totally dedicated to seeing the Gospel touch every part of the earth. Hell fears them.

This breed of Christians are, themselves, greatly blessed, refreshed, and anointed; yet, their main concern is not to have experiences with God or to be personally blessed. These believers are sometimes called "world Christians" because their one, overreaching goal is that every man, woman, boy, and girl in the world will hear the Gospel.

Let's consider how this "Great Commission" Church might look from hell's perspective.

The evangelization of the world and the return of Jesus means the beginning of the end for the devil. With this fact in mind, let's determine which activities and actions of the Church today make hell either rejoice or fear.

HELL REJOICES...

1. ...when the Church talks and behaves in a manner of inferiority, being fearful of the devil's end-time activities. Hell rejoices when believers have an excessive preoccupation with detailed end-time developments, the Antichrist, and the false prophet which paralyzes them from moving forward in the Great Commission. Hell laughs at believers sidetracked and preoccupied with interpreting and analyzing so-called "signs of the times," while forgetting about world evangelization.

2. ...when God's people become obsessed with and distracted by self-improvement courses, introverted personal prophecies, selfish interpretations of dreams and visions, meaningless predictions about the return of Jesus, etc. Anything that keeps the Church from fulfilling its mandate to bring in **the fullness of the Gentiles** will cause hell to revel.

The Bible does not say that the 144,000 or the Two Witnesses will complete the task of bringing in *the fullness of the Gentiles.*

3. ...at the popular teaching that the 144,000 saints of the tribes of Israel, or the Two Witnesses mentioned in the book of Revelation, are the ones who will complete the task of the Great Commission. The 144,000 are from the twelve tribes of Israel and serve a special purpose in God's plan for the nation of Israel. (See Revelation 7:14.)

   The Two Witnesses are special emissaries sent to Israel. (See Revelation 11:3.) The substance of their message is not revealed in the Bible, but a clue may be found in the fact that they are to be dressed in sackcloth. This could indicate that they will bring a message of repentance similar to that which John the Baptist preached.

   Clearly, neither the 144,000 nor the Two Witnesses have been commissioned to complete the task of bringing in the fullness of the Gentiles. This teaching, so prominently put forth by popular end-time prophecy teachers, does not have a shred of scriptural support. Furthermore, Jesus commanded no other group but the Church to carry out the task of evangelizing the world:

Then Jesus came and spoke to them, saying, "All authority has been given to Me in heaven and on earth.

"Go therefore and make disciples of all the nations, baptizing them in the name of the Father and of the Son and of the Holy Spirit,

"teaching them to observe all things that I have commanded you; and lo, I am with you always, even to the end of the age." Amen. Matthew 28:18-20

Speculative teachings about the 144,000 saints and the Two Witnesses in the book of Revelation only serve to neutralize the efforts of the Church and cause spiritual sluggishness.

In the book *The Challenge of Missions* its author, the late Dr. Oswald J. Smith, made the following statement,

> "I know of no theory that can do more to cut the nerve of missionary endeavour. Moreover, I know of no definite statement in the entire Bible that would lead me to believe, for one single moment, that the Jews are to evangelize the world during

The local church has no right to expend the tithe exclusively on itself.

If the local church considers itself unable to support missions, it should not call itself a church.

the days of the great tribulation, as some people seem to think."[1]

4. ...in the teaching which says that the tithe should be used exclusively on local church expenses. Yes, the Lord's tithe of our increase belongs to the local church. Yet, the local church has no right to expend the tithe exclusively on itself. The tithe should also be used for missions to the unreached, which is a divine mandate for each local church.

No church is too small for a missionary program. If the local church considers itself unable to support missions, it should not call itself a church. Rather, it should be a prayer group that is part of a church. If a local church is not involved in a regular missions program,

Statistics prove that 96 percent of all funds raised by the North American church stay in North America.

Out of the funds expended in overseas work, only a minor percentage is used to reach the unreached.

it is robbing its members of their very destiny and purpose as Christians.

5. ...in how Christians are sidetracked from the task of bringing in the fullness of the Gentiles by sensational and spiritual experiences that cause them only to look inward instead of becoming involved in the Great Commission.
6. ...when the myth is perpetuated that the world has already heard the Gospel, even though the most conservative estimates indicate that there are still 1.1 billion people who have never heard the name of Jesus. Many estimates put that figure as high as two billion.
7. ...in the myth that the Church has already given plenty of its money and effort to world missions. Statistics prove that 96 percent of all funds raised by the North American church stay in North America. Only 4 percent is actually used in overseas missions work. Note also that out of the funds expended in overseas work, only a minor percentage is used to

reach the unreached.[2] Most overseas efforts are expended in areas where the Gospel has been heard over and over again.

Dr. Oswald J. Smith said, "Why should anyone hear the Gospel twice before everyone has heard it once?"[3]

Hell fears...the church that spends more money on reaching the lost than it spends on buildings.

HELL FEARS...

1. ...the church that spends more money on reaching the lost than it spends on buildings.
2. ...the missionaries and missions organizations who, like Paul, search out the unreached areas and devote their time, finances, and efforts to penetrate those areas, rather than going where it is easy or where others have already gone.
3. ...the church and the believer who have as their one, overriding goal to rescue people from the jaws of hell and to populate heaven.
4. ...the believer who, like Paul, devotes priority time and resources to bring in the fullness of the Gentiles.

5. ...the church that dares to set as its goal at least 50 cents of every dollar to go to world missions.

6. ...the church and the believers who know their authority in the name of Jesus and fight fully armed in their spiritual armor. (See Ephesians 6:12-18.) This is the kind of church that will do more than teach a "cultural Christianity." It is a church that will preach that Jesus saves, heals, delivers, and baptizes in the Holy Spirit.

7. ...the church that, like the Antioch church (see Acts 13:1-4), is willing to commission its best people to missionary service, or the church that supports others who are commissioning missionaries.

What will it take for our generation to be the one which hears the last trumpet? What will it take for Jesus to come back in our lifetime? How can we participate in the Lord's return?

The answers are obvious:

- Take the Gospel to all ethnic groups. (See Matthew 24:14.)
- Bring in the fullness of the Gentiles. (See Romans 11:25.)
- Fulfill the sign of His return. (See Matthew 24:14.)

SECTION 3

HE IS COMING AT HARVEST TIME

CHAPTER 9

THE HARVEST

IMAGINE YOURSELF 10,000 YEARS INTO THE FUTURE. The Rapture of the Church is old news. The Millennium is long passed. The Church of Jesus Christ is in heaven. The devil is in the lake of fire.

The last biblical reference to the devil is found in Revelation, chapter 20.

> **The devil, who deceived them, was cast into the lake of fire and brimstone where the beast and the false prophet are. And they will be tormented day and night forever and ever.** **Revelation 20:10**

Compare this verse with the Bible's last reference to us, the believers:

> **And they shall reign forever and ever.**
> **Revelation 22:5**

Which place do you think will be the most populated — heaven or hell? Will the devil, although defeated, be thinking smugly that he has more people in the lake of fire than God has in heaven? Looking at society today, it may very well seem that would be the end result, except for the one great

> **Which place do you think will be the most populated — heaven or hell?**

prophetic event that will alter the spiritual landscape of the earth forever — *the harvest.*

It is very important that we understand the harvest and its connection to the sign of Jesus' return (which we will study in Chapter 15).

Jesus said, **"The harvest is the end of the age"** (Matthew 13:39). To better understand this outstanding (yet largely overlooked) event, let's look briefly at the symbolic significance of the three major Hebrew feasts. Although there are seven feasts, the following are considered major:

> **"Three times you shall keep a feast to Me in the year:**
>
> **"You shall keep the Feast of Unleavened Bread (you shall eat unleavened bread seven days, as I commanded you, at the time appointed in the month of Abib, for in it you came out of Egypt; none shall appear before Me empty);**
>
> **"and the Feast of Harvest, the firstfruits of your labors which you have sown in the field; and the Feast of Ingathering, which is at the end of the year, when you**

> **have gathered in the fruit of your labors from the field."** **Exodus 23:14-16**

The first major feast was that of Unleavened Bread, or the Feast of the Passover.

> **"'On the fourteenth day of the first month at twilight is the Lord's Passover.'"** **Leviticus 23:5**

Because the Passover was to be celebrated the first month of the year, it was known as the First Feast. Moses instituted the Passover around 1446 B.C., and for centuries Hebrew families celebrated this feast without fully understanding it. On the appointed day they would kill the selected Passover lamb, not yet knowing that its sacrifice was a prophetic act pointing forward to what Christ would do at Calvary.

It was not until approximately 750 years before Christ's birth that Isaiah applied the personal pronoun "he" to the lamb. Isaiah prophesied concerning the Messiah that ***He*** **was led as a lamb to the slaughter** (Isaiah 53:7).

Jesus, the Lamb of Calvary, died and rose again at Passover, according to the Old Testament Scriptures:

For I delivered to you...that Christ died for our sins according to the Scriptures,

and that He was buried, and that He rose again the third day according to the Scriptures.

1 Corinthians 15:3,4

Today we have an understanding of the Passover's significance that was unknown to the Hebrew people. Because the Passover celebration was prophetically fulfilled at Calvary, we have forgiveness for our sin, healing for our body, and freedom from pain, poverty, guilt, and shame. Calvary is our place of liberty and eternal life.

The second major feast was the Feast of Pentecost, or the Feast of Shavout, celebrated 50 days after Passover. Also known as the Feast of Firstfruits, it was the time when people expressed their thanksgiving to God for the first of the grain harvest and other crops:

"'Also on the day of the firstfruits, when you bring a new grain offering to the Lord at your Feast of Weeks, you shall have a holy convocation. You shall do no customary work.

"'You shall present a burnt offering as a sweet aroma to the Lord: two young bulls, one ram, and seven lambs in their first year,

They were actually performing an annual prophetic act, foreshadowing the day of Pentecost.

"'with their grain offering of fine flour mixed with oil: three-tenths of an ephah for each bull, two-tenths for the one ram,

"'and one-tenth for each of the seven lambs;

"'also one kid of the goats, to make atonement for you.

"'Be sure they are without blemish. You shall present them with their drink offerings, besides the regular burnt offering with its grain offering.'"

Numbers 28:26-31

Again, Hebrew families celebrated this feast for centuries without fully understanding its significance. They were actually performing an annual prophetic act, foreshadowing the day of Pentecost which would come.

When we celebrate Pentecost on the Christian calendar today, we do it with hindsight's advantage. We remember the outpouring of the Holy Spirit and the "firstfruits" of the spiritual harvest of the Church when 3,000 were saved on the first day of Pentecost. As great as these numbers seem, the Bible tells us that these are only the **firstfruits**, an indication that something greater is yet to come.

Harvest time goes beyond merely gathering the firstfruits.

Unlike in the Old Testament, where the Holy Spirit came upon individuals, believers today have the Holy Spirit living inside them. They can be baptized in the Spirit with the evidence of speaking in tongues, and have the gifts of the Spirit flowing through them. Thank God for the blessing of the Feast of Pentecost!

Yet, all the blessings believers personally experience are not the full work of the Holy Spirit. There is a greater work of the Holy Spirit about to be done on the earth — the harvest is coming.

The third major feast was the Feast of Ingathering, sometimes referred to as the Feast of Harvest, or the Feast of Tabernacles. During this great religious celebration, the Israelites commemorated the wilderness years of wandering before they entered the promised land:

> **"You shall observe the Feast of Tabernacles seven days, when you have gathered from your threshing floor and from your winepress.**
>
> **"And you shall rejoice in your feast, you and your son and your daughter, your male servant and your female**

servant and the Levite, the stranger and the fatherless and the widow, who are within your gates.

"Seven days you shall keep a sacred feast to the Lord your God in the place which the Lord chooses, because the Lord your God will bless you in all your produce and in all the work of your hands, so that you surely rejoice.

"Three times a year all your males shall appear before the Lord your God in the place which He chooses: at the Feast of Unleavened Bread, at the Feast of Weeks, and at the Feast of Tabernacles; and they shall not appear before the Lord empty-handed.

"Every man shall give as he is able, according to the blessing of the Lord your God which He has given you." Deuteronomy 16:13-17

In observing this feast, the people lived for seven days in temporary shelters made of tree branches. This was to relive and remember their experience as a people with no permanent dwellings, as wanderers in the wilderness:

"'You shall dwell in booths for seven days. All who are native Israelites shall dwell in booths.'"

Leviticus 23:42

The Feast of the Harvest took place **"at the end of the year, when** [they had] **gathered in the fruit of** [their] **labors**

from the field" (Exodus 23:16). In the book of Leviticus, we read that the Feast of Tabernacles would be celebrated **"when** [they had] **gathered in the fruit of the land"** (Leviticus 23:39). The seven days of rejoicing would take place only when they had brought all the harvest into the barns. The Feast of Ingathering or Feast of Tabernacles was to take place at the end of the agricultural year.

Again, the nation of Israel celebrated this feast for centuries without fully understanding its meaning. The Feast of Harvest also embodied a prophetic foreshadowing of a significant event in God's plan for humanity. It spoke of a time when all the spiritual fruit of the earth (Jew and Gentile) would be ingathered. This has not yet occurred. Just as many lived in the time before the fulfillment of the feasts of Passover and Pentecost, we now live in a time preceding the full manifestation of the Feast of Harvest.

Some teach that the Feast of Harvest is symbolic of the millennial reign of Christ. My point is not to argue with this interpretation, but rather to demonstrate that it took place at the end of the harvest year. In a New Testament context, the Feast of Harvest cannot take place until the spiritual harvest of the fullness of the Gentiles, brought into God's kingdom, has taken place. (See Romans 11:25.)

The spiritual harvest of the earth must take place before the feast of the millennial reign of Christ can begin. Since the Bible is abundantly clear that it is the Church and no one else who will fulfill the Great Commission, this must all take place during the Church Age. Jesus said, **"The harvest is the end of the age"** (Matthew 13:39).

The signs of the approaching harvest time are all around us. Yet there are still over one billion who have never heard — even once — the name of Jesus.

We can be sure that the harvest is coming. Just as the Feast of Passover was fulfilled at Calvary and the Feast of Pentecost was fulfilled in the Upper Room, so also will the Feast of Ingathering (Harvest) be fulfilled.

Get ready for the fulfillment of one of the greatest prophecies of the Bible. There will be a great ingathering into God's kingdom. All the earth will hear the Gospel. The harvest will affect you, your family, your city, and your country.

CHAPTER 10

JESUS' PROPHECIES ABOUT THE HARVEST

IN MATTHEW 13:24-29, JESUS TELLS THE PARABLE of the wheat and the tares and how they grow side by side. Concluding the parable, Jesus says,

> **"Let both grow together until the harvest, and at the time of harvest I will say to the reapers, 'First gather together the tares and bind them in bundles to burn them, but gather the wheat into my barn.'"**
>
> **Matthew 13:30**

His words indicate the wheat and the tares will co-exist **until the harvest.**

I love when Jesus explains His own sermon, as He did when He was alone with His disciples. They asked Him, **"Explain to us the parable of the tares of the field"** (Matthew 13:36).

> **"He answered and said to them: "He who sows the good seed is the Son of Man.**
>
> **"The field is the world, the good seeds are the sons of the kingdom, but the tares are the sons of the wicked one.**

> **"The enemy who sowed them is the devil, the harvest is the end of the age, and the reapers are the angels.**
>
> **"Therefore as the tares are gathered and burned in the fire, so it will be at the end of this age."**
>
> **Matthew 13:37-40**

Jesus clearly said:

- **the field is the world — the harvest is the end of the age.**
- the harvest is two-fold: **the sons of the kingdom** and **the sons of the wicked one.**

Many have viewed this scripture verse only in a negative way, seeing it as a prophecy of God's judgment on unbelievers. However, I see in this scripture the promise that there will be **sons of the kingdom** found throughout all the world.

The harvest will not be limited to one geographical area. In our century we have heard wonderful reports of spiritual harvests and revivals in certain areas of the earth, such as Nagaland in northeastern India, the island of Timor in Indonesia, and South Korea. While these reports are wonderful, their scope is limited to certain areas. The end of the age that Jesus speaks of will be a worldwide ingathering of unprecedented proportions.

If the entire world is to be harvested as Jesus says, then His statement that the harvest **is the end of the age** (Matthew 13:39) clearly ties in with His words in

Mark 13:10: **And the gospel must first be preached to all the nations.**

We have already explained that the word "nations" is the Greek word *ethnos* meaning "any group of people distinguished by race, language, and/or culture." The Gospel witness must first be established in each one of the world's 20,000-plus identifiable ethnic groups. A worldwide, spiritual harvest time means that all the earth — all nations (tribes) and ethnicities, every man, woman, boy, and girl — will be reached. Clearly, the end of the age will be characterized by intense evangelization.

It is important to distinguish between the words "age" and "world." The Greek word for "age" is *aion,*[1] while the Greek word *kosmos*[2] means "world." Some translators have incorrectly translated the word *aion* used in the gospel of Matthew as "world," claiming that Jesus said the harvest is the end of the world, and thus, the disciples' question in Matthew 24:3 would be, "What will be the sign of the end of the world?"

This is incorrect. Jesus' teaching does not concern the end of the world, but rather, the end of the age — **this age.**

The Greek word for "age" is *aion,* while the Greek word *kosmos* means "world."

Obviously, Jesus is teaching about the age that His resurrection would soon usher in, the age of the preaching of the Gospel.

Jesus continues teaching on the end of this age, saying,

> **"Again, the kingdom of heaven is like a dragnet that was cast into the sea and gathered some of every kind,**
>
> **"which, when it was full, they drew to shore; and they sat down and gathered the good into vessels, but threw the bad away.**
>
> **"So it will be at the end of the age. The angels will come forth,** [and] **separate the wicked from among the just."** **Matthew 13:47-49**

Notice the phrase, **so it will be at the end of the age** (v. 49). Here, the illustration is not given in agricultural language, as with the wheat and tares parable. Instead, Jesus uses an example from a fisherman's experience.

The kingdom of God:

- will be like a **dragnet.**
- will gather **some of every kind.**
- will be **full.**

While there is an obvious emphasis here on a separation between the **good** and the **bad,** there is also an emphasis on **some of every kind.** While there will be some of every kind among those who will be separated from God, at the

Chapter 13 relates to Chapter 24, in that they both deal with the end of the age.

end of the age there will be a spiritual ingathering of people that will also include **some of every kind.** The Gospel will not just touch specially favored countries in Africa, Asia, South America, or North America. It will gather every kind. It will touch Saudi Arabia, Libya, Algeria, Morocco, Madagascar, France, Afghanistan, the Middle East, northern India — yes, every area which has, until now, been considered "hard" to reach with the Gospel.

It is important that we view the gospel of Matthew's end-time teaching in its entirety. Chapter 13 relates to chapter 24, in that they both deal with the end of the age. The prerequisite for the coming of the Lord is that the Gospel of the kingdom be preached in all the world; Jesus prophesied a great harvest at the end of the age. There is a clear connection between these two facts.

Without a worldwide spiritual harvest, the Church will not be able to fulfill Matthew 24:14, and without the fulfillment of Matthew 24:14, the Lord cannot come back.

Some may argue that the separation between the **good** and the **bad** refers to the final judgment. Undoubtedly this is so, but my point here is to focus on the fact that **some of**

every kind are represented among the **good.** This simply means that the Gospel will have gone to every tribe, tongue, and nation.

The mandate to accomplish this task has been given, *not* to angels, *not* to the nation of Israel, *not* to the Two Witnesses in the book of Revelation, but rather to the Church and the Church alone:

> **And Jesus came and spoke to them, saying, "All authority has been given to Me in heaven and on earth.**
>
> **"Go therefore and make disciples of all the nations, baptizing them in the name of the Father and of the Son and of the Holy Spirit,**
>
> **"teaching them to observe all things that I have commanded you; and lo, I am with you always, even to the end of the age." Amen. Matthew 28:18-20**

CHAPTER 11

END-TIME MYTHS

WHEN A YOUNG MAN LOOKS FOR A SUITABLE WIFE, the woman of his dreams, old-age nursing homes or hospitals for the chronically ill are not the places he will frequent. Instead, he will look in a place where he can find a bride who is full of life and health.

The Church of Jesus Christ is the Bride of Christ. However, some give the impression that the end-time Church is an emaciated and lifeless bride, barely having strength to make it to the end.

This picture of the Church has fostered an end-time theology which portrays the devil as a very large force and Jesus as a mere rescuer of His Church from the earth's troubles.

This picture of the Church has fostered an end-time theology which portrays the devil as a very large force and Jesus as a mere rescuer of His Church from the earth's troubles.

Give Jesus some credit! He is not returning in all of His glory for a chronically sick, emaciated, timid, or defeated Church.

Give Jesus some credit! He is not returning in all of His glory for a chronically sick, emaciated, timid, or defeated Church. Just as a young bridegroom looks for a bride with life and vitality, Jesus, the Bridegroom of all bridegrooms, is coming back for a life-producing, vibrant bride. (See Ephesians 5:27.)

Let's carefully study some of the scripture verses that have been misused to support the negative end-time myths.

MYTH NUMBER ONE:

ONLY A FEW WILL BE SAVED BECAUSE THE GATE IS "NARROW."

In the Christian, evangelical environment in which I grew up, an artist's depiction of two parallel roads served as a portrayal of life. One road was very narrow, and only a few people would walk along it. Alongside it was a road called the "broad way." It appeared both appealing and glittering, and thousands crowded along it. When one examined the two roads, the narrow road became narrower as it led upward and eventually ended in a burst of light and glory, symbolic of heaven. In contrast, the broad way led into a dark void, and the thousands who crowded it fell over a cliff and into an abyss of fire.

I remember looking at this depiction. To my young, impressionable mind it seemed to mean that only a few people would know Jesus. Of course, this concept was based upon the scripture verses in which Jesus said:

> **"Enter by the narrow gate; for wide is the gate and broad is the way that leads to destruction, and there are many who go in by it.**
>
> **"Because narrow is the gate and difficult is the way which leads to life, and there are few who find it."**
>
> **Matthew 7:13,14**

This verse has been used to teach that only a remnant will make it to heaven. Let's look carefully at what Jesus said. First of all, note that here Jesus was addressing His teaching to those who followed the Jewish Law and the prophets — and there were many of those in attendance. Jesus was the Messiah, and the **way which leads to life.** Through the centuries of Jewish history, relatively few Jews have found Jesus Christ as their Messiah. Many Jews have walked through **the wide gate,** just as Jesus said they would.

However, in the last few years, there have been increasing numbers of Jewish people receiving Jesus as their Messiah. This surge in Messianic Jewry has brought about great debate in Jewish communities, especially within the state of modern Israel. I believe the day is fast approaching when all Israel will be saved. (See Romans 11:26.) The increase in the number of Messianic Jews is a further indication that we are approaching the coming of the Lord.

Moreover, when we look at the past 2,000 years of Gentile world history, we clearly see that Jesus' statement that only a **few** will find **the way which leads to life** describes what has already transpired throughout the centuries. In fact, most of the time period between the day of Pentecost and today has been characterized by spiritual darkness.

The Dark Ages was a period in European history from about A.D. 400 to the 16th-century Reformation when very few people even knew how to be saved. The institutionalized Church of Rome allowed only priests to read the Bible.

The increase in the number of Messianic Jews is a further indication that we are approaching the coming of the Lord.

Of this period we can certainly say that only a "few" found the way that leads to eternal life.

However, neither the history of the past 2,000 years nor these verses in Matthew, chapter 7, in any way diminish the truth of a great end-time harvest. At the end of the age, there will be a spiritual acceleration. The Church's missionary program will shift from first gear into overdrive. The end of the age is harvest time; it will affect all flesh — the Jews as well as the Gentiles. The end time will not be business as usual — it's harvest time!

Paul spoke of the salvation of the Jewish nation. He said that all the nation of Israel would be saved — after **the fullness of the Gentiles has come in** (Romans 11:25).

The King of kings of the Gentiles and the Messiah of the Jews is one and the same person — Jesus Christ.

This is not the place to do a full commentary on Romans, chapter 11. It will suffice to summarize a few major points of this important chapter.

God's plan for an end-time harvest includes the nation of Israel. The King of kings of the Gentiles and the Messiah of the Jews is one and the same person — Jesus Christ. God has a harvest plan for the Gentile world, discussed in detail in this book. He also has a harvest plan for the Jewish nation. God has not cast away His people (see Romans 11:1); however, their full salvation cannot come until **the fullness of the Gentiles has come in** (Romans 11:25). Once this Gentile harvest has been accomplished, there will be a great day of salvation when all of natural Israel will see Jesus as their Messiah:

"And I will pour on the house of David and on the inhabitants of Jerusalem the Spirit of grace and supplication; then they will look on Me whom they have pierced. Yes, they will mourn for Him as one mourns for his only son, and grieve for Him as one grieves for a firstborn.

"In that day there shall be a great mourning in Jerusalem, like the mourning at Hadad Rimmon in the plain of Megiddo.

"In that day a fountain shall be opened for the house of David and for the inhabitants of Jerusalem, for sin and for uncleanness." Zechariah 12:10,11;13:1

Yes, God has an end-time harvest plan for natural Israel and an end-time harvest plan for the world. These two plans are intricately interwoven in that the salvation of natural Israel cannot come about until **the fullness of the Gentiles has come in** (Romans 11:25).

Re-examine Jesus' statement about the "narrow" gate and the "broad" way. Admittedly, throughout history the cause of world evangelization has moved along relatively slowly. Many have walked along the "broad" way that leads to destruction. All this will change during the time period Jesus calls "the harvest." There will no longer be just a few coming through the "narrow" gate or the "difficult" way. The end of this age will signify a great spiritual awakening.

Heaven's "dragnet" of people will be "full." (See Matthew 13:47-49.)

As we approach the end of the age, there will be an acceleration — it's harvest time!

MYTH NUMBER TWO:

WHEN JESUS COMES BACK ONLY A FEW WILL BE FOUND FAITHFUL.

> **"Nevertheless, when the Son of Man comes, will He really find faith on the earth?"** **Luke 18:8**

The correct answer is "no," because when the Son of Man comes back to rule and reign on the earth, the Church will have been caught up! For a short time the Antichrist and the false prophet will dominate the earth. Those who refuse to take the mark of the Antichrist will be oppressed and killed. Under these dire circumstances, there will indeed be little faith found on the earth:

> [The Antichrist] **causes all, both small and great, rich and poor, free and slave, to receive a mark on their right hand or on their foreheads,**
>
> **and that no one may buy or sell except one who has the mark or the name of the beast, or the number of his name.** **Revelation 13:16,17**

The earth will be seduced into worshiping the image of the Antichrist:

> **Then a third angel followed them, saying with a loud voice, "If anyone worships the beast and his image, and receives his mark on his forehead or on his hand,..."** **Revelation 14:9**

When Jesus returns with His saints to the Mount of Olives, it is not to find faith — He will come to do battle:

> **"These will make war with the Lamb, and the Lamb will overcome them, for He is Lord of lords and King of kings; and those who are with Him are called, chosen, and faithful."** **Revelation 17:14**

At His coming on the Mount of Olives, Jesus will destroy those who destroy the earth:

> **"...and should destroy those who destroy the earth."**
> **Revelation 11:18**

The final war is further described in Revelation, chapters 19 and 20, which ends with Satan being bound for 1,000 years.

> **Luke 18:8 must be understood in the light of its proper biblical chronology.**

The fulfillment of Matthew 24:14 takes place first, followed by the Church being caught up to meet the Lord in the air. After this, the Lord returns with His saints to the earth, where the Antichrist and the false prophet have been ruling.

Verse 8 in Luke, chapter 18, must not be used to perpetuate a doctrine that teaches that the Church will be weak, emaciated, or defunct in the end time. This verse must be understood in the light of its proper biblical chronology as an obvious reference to what takes place *after* the fulfillment of Matthew 24:14.

MYTH NUMBER THREE:

THE LOVE OF MOST WILL WAX COLD.

Another scripture verse used to support a negative view of the end time is Matthew 24:12:

> **"And because lawlessness will abound, the love of many will grow cold."**

Please note that it does not say "the love of most," but **the love of many.**

I remember hearing sermons based on this verse, with the emphasis leading one to think only a few God-fearing people would be waiting for Jesus to return. The difference between "most" and "many" must be underlined before this verse can be properly understood.

Let me give you an example. In 1991, I preached to an estimated 250,000 people in a single service in Sofia, Bulgaria. This estimate is based on aerial photography by the Bulgarian police. Two hundred and fifty thousand is "many" people. However, Sofia's population is almost one million. Therefore, "most" of the citizens were not present at that service.

Yes, the love of "many" will grow cold, but "many" is not the same as "most." While there will be "many" who turn their backs on God, the Gospel will still be **preached in all the world,** and Matthew 24:14 will be fulfilled. **Many will wax cold** in their love, but that still leaves an opportunity for "most" to love God.

MYTH NUMBER FOUR:

THERE WILL BE A GREAT FALLING AWAY IN THE CHURCH IN THE END TIME.

There has been a lot of teaching in the modern Church about the great "falling away." In fact, the Bible clearly speaks of two periods of "falling away," one in the Church, which has already occurred, and the other in the world,

The Bible clearly speaks of two periods of "falling away."

which is currently occurring. It was Paul who predicted the falling away within the Church:

> **"For I know this, that after my departure savage wolves will come in among you, not sparing the flock.**
>
> **"Also from among yourselves men will rise up, speaking perverse things, to draw away the disciples after themselves." Acts 20:29,30**

Similarly, the apostle Peter wrote of destructive heresies and false prophets infiltrating the people of God:

> **But there were also false prophets among the people, even as there will be false teachers among you, who will secretly bring in destructive heresies, even denying the Lord who bought them, and bring on themselves swift destruction.**
>
> **And many will follow their destructive ways, because of whom the way of truth will be blasphemed.**
>
> **By covetousness they will exploit you with deceptive words; for a long time their judgment has not been idle, and their destruction does not slumber.**
>
> **2 Peter 2:1-3**

Paul warned Timothy:

> **Now the Spirit expressly says that in latter times some will depart from the faith, giving heed to deceiving spirits and doctrines of demons,**
>
> **speaking lies in hypocrisy, having their own conscience seared with a hot iron,**
>
> **forbidding to marry, and commanding to abstain from foods which God created to be received with thanksgiving by those who believe and know the truth.**
>
> **1 Timothy 4:1-3**

These are only a few New Testament scriptures that speak of perilous times within the Church.

This great falling away in the Church became apparent in the third century A.D. and intensified until the 16th century. Under the rule of the Roman emperor Constantine in the fourth century, the Church's situation was elevated

It was believed that the grace of God could be obtained through...sacraments.

from a state of persecution to one of great acceptance. Eventually, Christianity became the state religion.

In fact, within a few years after Christianity became the state religion, a law decreed that one had to be a follower of the Christian religion in order to be employed in the Roman civil service. This did great damage to the cause of Christianity. Consequently, one's love for God was not the only motive for church involvement; it was now a necessary means to further one's career. Christianity was not only accepted by the government, it was favored. Gone were the days when Christians who held on to their faith were thrown to the lions.

Furthermore, institutionalized "Christianity" removed the focus from personal relationship with Jesus, and placed an emphasis on the receiving of sacraments. It was believed that the grace of God could be obtained through these ritualistic sacraments rather than by being born again. Each sacrament was supposed to impart the grace of God to a person. Eventually, the focus completely shifted away from Jesus' finished work at Calvary.

People were not allowed to read the Bible themselves, as the clergy had monopolized this area. Also, the Church's spiritual decline continued as pagan tradition crept in. By the 14th, 15th, and 16th centuries, the Church had regressed so far that salvation could be purchased in the open marketplace by merely making a donation. The Church literally sold square inches of heavenly territory to its wealthy parishioners. This period of almost 1,300 years can certainly be described as a "great falling away."

During all these centuries, a remnant of people, often referred to as "sects," had to earnestly contend for the faith against religious opposition and man-made traditions:

> **Beloved, while I was very diligent to write to you concerning our common salvation, I found it necessary to write to you exhorting you to contend earnestly for the faith which was once for all delivered to the saints.**
>
> **Jude 1:3**

To even comprehend the magnitude of how low the Church had fallen, we must understand that the Roman Catholic Church in the 16th century had become the most powerful institution in the world. It controlled education, morality, and politics. Its standard stood indisputable. If anyone dared to contradict or even question the Church's teaching, he was declared a heretic. The masses had become so deceived that one 16th-century reformer wrote:

> "The laity set aside the Word of God, and they heed their clergy, right or wrong. If the clergy in their seductive way were to tell the laity that the devil, or an ass, is God, they will believe that too."[1]

Reformational preachers like Calvin, Luther, Wycliffe, Hus, and Savanorola were raised up by God to declare forgotten biblical truths. These 15th- and 16th-century preachers brought revelation to the simple biblical fact that we are justified by faith in Jesus.

Later, men like John and Charles Wesley and the early Methodists restored the truth of sanctification to the Church. William Booth and the Salvation Army highlighted truths about personal soulwinning. The British shoe cobbler, William Carey, and the early Moravians brought the challenge of world missions into focus.

Each of these revival and reformational movements throughout the past five centuries brought restoration and began to reverse the effects of the great falling away in the Church.

The 20th century began with the outpouring of the Holy Spirit at Azusa Street in 1906. Since then, we have seen a tremendous period of restoration. Truths that have not been preached for centuries have been brought to the forefront: the authority of the believer; divine healing for the body; the gifts of the Spirit for every believer; praise and worship; the function of the apostle, prophet, evangelist, pastor, and teacher in the Church; etc.

We are a very blessed people to be able to enjoy biblical truths that have been hidden for generations. The great falling away in the Church is over. This is the day of restoration.

It is not merely the Antichrist, but a spirit of the Antichrist...

MYTH NUMBER FIVE :

BECAUSE OF THE EVIL INFLUENCE IN THE END TIME, ONLY A FEW CAN POSSIBLY BE SAVED.

Yes, there will be evil in the end time — a second great falling away — not in the Church, but in the world. Paul wrote the Thessalonian church to inform them of what would take place before the coming of the Lord:

> **Let no one deceive you by any means; for that Day will not come unless the falling away comes first, and the man of sin is revealed, the son of perdition,**
>
> **who opposes and exalts himself above all that is called God or that is worshiped, so that he sits as God in the temple of God, showing himself that he is God.**
>
> **2 Thessalonians 2:3,4**

This is an obvious reference to the AntiChrist. Paul then went on to say,

> **For the mystery of lawlessness is already at work; only He who now restrains will do so until He is taken out of the way.** **2 Thessalonians 2:7**

It is not merely the Antichrist, but a spirit of the Antichrist, which is released upon the earth: **For the mystery of lawlessness is already at work.** This spirit of the Antichrist is accompanied by **powers, signs, lying wonders,** and **unrighteous deception.** (See 2 Thessalonians 2:9,10.)

John says that this Antichrist spirit has already gone into the world: **And this is the spirit of the Antichrist, which you have heard was coming, and is now already in the world** (1 John 4:3). The Church is the restraining power that holds back the full force of this rampant spirit of lawlessness: **Only He who now restrains will do so until He is taken out of the way** (2 Thessalonians 2:7).

We currently are living in this period of a great falling away in the world. This is a time of polarization. While the glory of God is increasing in the Church and the fulfillment of Matthew 24:14 is certain, correlatively, there is a vicious outpouring of the spirit of hell, with unprecedented lawlessness and ungodliness on the earth. No wonder the last chapter of the Bible says,

> **"He who is unjust, let him be unjust still; he who is filthy, let him be filthy still; he who is righteous, let him be righteous still; he who is holy, let him be holy still."**
>
> **Revelation 22:11**

As we approach the end of the age, two parallel events will play out on earth: the great falling away in the world, and a great, worldwide ingathering of people into the Church.

While the world will become increasingly evil, the Church will be strong, full of life and vitality. It will be **a glorious church, not having spot or wrinkle or any such thing, but...holy and without blemish** (Ephesians 5:27).

In Chapter 14 we will see how this ingathering has already started. The worldwide, born-again Church is growing at an unprecedented rate. Jesus is coming back for a glorious bride who **has made herself ready.**

> **"Let us be glad and rejoice and give Him glory, for the marriage of the Lamb has come, and His wife has made herself ready."** **Revelation 19:7**

CHAPTER 12

END-TIME ACCELERATION

WE ARE APPROACHING THE MOST INTENSE PERIOD in human history. In Luke, chapter 14, one of those listening to Jesus' teaching said to Him,

> **"Blessed is he who shall eat bread in the kingdom of God!"** **Luke 14:15**

This seems like a strange statement, and one may wonder what the man was referring to. In its context, the only logical conclusion would be that his statement referred to what is known as "the marriage supper of the Lamb." This is a supper that has been planned by God for thousands of years and will take place when the Church has been caught up to meet the Lord.

The person who spoke to Jesus in this verse had it right, because those who will be at that supper will be blessed indeed!

> **Then he said to me, "Write: 'Blessed are those who are called to the marriage supper of the Lamb!'"**
> **Revelation 19:9**

Jesus responded to the man's statement by telling a parable, which is a very important reference in understanding the end time. As we study this passage of teaching, think about what it means for your family and friends.

> **Then He said to him, "A certain man gave a great supper and invited many,**
>
> **"and sent his servant at supper time to say to those who were invited, 'Come, for all things are now ready.'**
>
> **"But they all with one accord began to make excuses....**
>
> **"So that servant came and reported these things to his master. Then the master of the house, being angry, said to his servant, 'Go out quickly into the streets and lanes of the city, and bring in here the poor and the maimed and the lame and the blind.'**
>
> **"And the servant said, 'Master, it is done as you commanded, and still there is room.'**
>
> **"Then the master said to the servant, 'Go out into the highways and hedges, and compel them to come in, that my house may be filled.**
>
> **"'For I say to you that none of those men who were invited shall taste my supper.'" Luke 14:16-18,21-24**

Notice that a general invitation to the great supper had already been extended to **many** (v. 16). Since Jesus gave the Great Commission on the Mount of Olives, the invitation to repent and believe the Good News has gone out to "many." Missionaries have taught the Gospel, and many even have given their lives for the sake of preaching it.

Although the light of the Gospel has periodically been dimmed, it has never gone out completely, and today hundreds of millions confess Jesus Christ as their Lord and Savior. The invitation to come to Christ, which has gone out for the past 2,000 years, has reached many.

After the general invitation, Jesus spoke of repeated invitations at **supper time.** Suddenly, something happened. There was an acceleration; the servants became busy reissuing the invitation.

The reason for this acceleration was that people *had to* respond. Time was running out. They had to heed the invitation, **"Come, for all things are now ready"** (Luke 14:17).

I believe that, according to God's prophetic calendar, we are now at "supper time." Today there is an urgency as never before to get the Gospel out.

Jesus went on to teach about how those invited made excuses, to which the master of the house responded by saying,

> **"'Go out quickly into the streets and lanes of the city, and bring in here the poor and the maimed and the lame and the blind.'"** **Luke 14:21**

The servant then complained to the master, **"Still there is room"** (v. 22). Jesus stressed that there should be no room remaining. The house had to be **full.** This reiterates what He said in the gospel of Matthew, the **"...dragnet...was full"** (Matthew 13:47,48). It also ties in with the words of the apostle Paul in Romans 11:25, that the fullness of the Gentiles must come in.

The master then issued the third command to the servant,

> **"'Go out into the highways and hedges, and compel them to come in, that my house may be filled.'"**
>
> **Luke 14:23**

Notice the acceleration. At first, the servant was to **say** (v. 17). Then he was to **bring in** (v. 21), and finally, he was to **compel** (v. 23).

The word "say" is the Greek word *epo,* which means "to speak, bring word, tell."[1]

"Bring in" is the Greek word *eisago,* which means "to lead."[2]

"Compel" is the Greek word *anagkazo,* which means "to oblige, to constrain, to cause to act."[3]

Even though an invitation to accept Christ has been issued for more than 1,900 years, at "supper time" the call will increase in strength.

> **Something will grip people's hearts "causing them to take action."**

First, the invitation will be reissued. Then, there will be an outpouring of God's Spirit to the degree that it will be as if people are "guided, taken by the hand," and "led" into the kingdom of God.

Finally, in the closing hours of the Church's mission on earth, there will be such an outpouring of God's Spirit, it will be like a great compelling "force." Something will grip people's hearts "causing them to take action" to receive Christ, even if they previously have been opponents of the Gospel. This ties in with the truth about the harvest prophesied by Jesus.

Jesus closed the parable with these words,

> **"'For I say to you that none of those men who were invited shall taste my supper.'" Luke 14:24**

It seems this final ingathering of people to the marriage supper of the Lamb will be an unprecedented outpouring of God's Spirit upon the lost. Jesus' statement implies that many religious people will miss it, while the poor, the maimed, the lame, and the blind, and those on the "highways" and "byways" of life will be brought in.

The objective from the Master's viewpoint is that the house must be full. There will not be any empty seats in heaven. Our heavenly Father dislikes empty places. Similarly, every man and woman of God detests reports of Church decline.

I am an ardent reader of many of the leading denominational newspapers. Quite often, there are reports and statements which indicate the critical situation in which some of these churches find themselves. A steady decline in membership and attendance is most often the problem. Whenever I read a report along these lines, something rises up within me in protest.

Our heavenly Father's attitude is that the house must be full.

- The dragnet will be *full.*
- The *full*ness of the Gentiles will come in.
- Heaven will be *full* of people.

CHAPTER 13

THE ELEVENTH HOUR

HAVE YOU EVER HEARD THE EXPRESSION that we are living in a time that could be described, prophetically, as one minute to midnight? I hesitate to set exact timings, but certainly, I don't question that we are in the eleventh hour, prophetically speaking. In Matthew, chapter 20, Jesus told a parable that sheds unusual insight into what will happen in the eleventh hour of Church history:

> **"For the kingdom of heaven is like a landowner who went out early in the morning to hire laborers for his vineyard.**
>
> **"Now when he had agreed with the laborers for a denarius a day, he sent them into his vineyard.**
>
> **"And he went out about the third hour and saw others standing idle in the marketplace,**
>
> **"and said to them, 'You also go into the vineyard, and whatever is right I will give you.' So they went.**
>
> **"Again he went out about the sixth and the ninth hour, and did likewise.**

"And about the eleventh hour he went out and found others standing idle, and said to them, 'Why have you been standing here idle all day?'

"They said to him, 'Because no one hired us.' He said to them, 'You also go into the vineyard, and whatever is right you will receive.'

"So when evening had come, the owner of the vineyard said to his steward, 'Call the laborers and give them their wages, beginning with the last to the first.'

"And when those came who were hired about the eleventh hour, they each received a denarius."

Matthew 20:1-9

The landowner hired some laborers early in the morning. He then hired more at the third hour, more at the sixth hour, and more again at the ninth hour. Finally, he added a large number to his workforce at the eleventh hour.

The common emphasis in teaching this parable is that all the workers received the same wage regardless of what hour they had begun their labor; God will reward each one as He sees fit.

There is another truth in this parable: if more laborers were added at each time interval, it stands to reason that the eleventh hour's labor force was the greatest. Therefore, a greater harvest would be reaped at the last hour than any other hour of the workday.

I believe the eleventh hour of Church history is the time when the greatest evangelism work in world history will be carried out. More laborers than ever before will be busy accomplishing the task of carrying the Gospel to the masses who have not yet heard it.

Let's illustrate this truth through a modern-day sports event. In a Stanley Cup ice hockey final, the players don't complain about being on the roster for the final game of the season. On the contrary, they are excited to be on a team contending for the coveted cup.

Similarly, it would be ludicrous to think that during the last quarter of a Super Bowl game, suddenly the football

The Church of Jesus Christ has entered the "playoffs" of human history.

players decide to quit or go to the dressing room. Quite the opposite. The playoff season in any sport is a time of intensification, of doing more and playing harder than ever before. The coach pulls out all stops, and each player endeavors to break through to higher levels of achievement.

The Church of Jesus Christ has entered the "playoffs" of human history. Certainly, this is not the time to rest on our laurels or to be worldly-minded. This is the time for an intensified labor of bringing in the harvest of the earth.

If we are in the eleventh hour of human history, the last trumpet will soon sound and our task will be complete. We should not quit now, but rather we should work with ever-increasing intensity.

I am writing this chapter while traveling home from a pastors' seminar in Delhi, India. More than 2,000 pastors participated, and the Holy Spirit moved in an unusual way. Leaders were challenged to take the Gospel to the 635,000 Indian towns and villages where, as of yet, there is no Christian witness.

There were two unique altar calls during this seminar. At the first call, more than 1,000 pastors made a promise before God that before the end of the current year they would go to one of the unreached towns in India and plant a church. At the second altar call, the invitation was given to those who would be willing to be a part of one of 100 apostolic teams that would each plant 100 new churches in the next ten years.

As far as I could tell, every pastor in the seminar responded to that second call. The given challenge was to focus especially on the unreached states of India where the church is almost completely unnoticed, such as the states of Rajasthan, Haryana, Gujarat, Uttar Pradesh, to name a few.

I believe this is the eleventh hour of Church history. The labor force in India and worldwide is increasing. More people than ever before are about to be brought into God's kingdom.

CHAPTER 14

SEVEN SIGNS OF THE HARVEST

IT IS ONE THING TO NOTE THE PROPHETIC WORDS spoken in Scripture and quite another to see the actual fulfillment of those prophecies right before our eyes. There are signs that the harvest of the earth has already intensified. Rejoice as you examine the following seven indicators.

SIGN NUMBER ONE:

A CHANGE IN THE SPIRITUAL CLIMATE

During the past 200 years, philosophers from Voltaire to Marx taught that Bible-based Christian religion would eventually disappear, certainly by the end of the 20th century. They contended that science, technology, and industry would pave the way for an era of great "enlightenment" in which human reason, rather than religious beliefs, would govern people's lives.

As late as the 1960s, it seemed as if they might be right. The "God-is-dead" philosophy was prevalent in many parts of the world, reaching its height in the early 1970s.

But since then, many newspapers, magazines, and studies have all, in various forms, indicated a surprising trend: the end of this century has marked a return to faith and spiritual beliefs. One leading Canadian publication, *Maclean's*, writes,

> Mainstream North America is on a massive spiritual quest, sampling a smorgasbord of eastern and metaphysical beliefs in search of psychological assurances that materialism has failed to provide. There are signs that, far from being just another baby boom fad, it represents a significant shift away from mainstream religion.[1]

To some, this renewed spiritual interest has negative connotations, appearing to draw people away from biblical Christianity into "New Age" or eastern religions. I see it as a positive development. While it is true that some have entered into "New Age" philosophies, this trend shows that people are skeptical of established, institutionalized religion. Their hearts are open to the supernatural realm, including the supernatural Gospel, like never before. This environment of spiritual hunger correlates with Jesus' prophecies of the "harvest at the end of the age."

This present "end-of-the-age" generation is ready to be spiritually impacted. It is ripe for the Gospel.

This present "end-of-the-age" generation is ready to be spiritually impacted.

SIGN NUMBER TWO:

THE RISE OF SPIRIT-FILLED CHURCHES

For the past 450 years, Christianity has basically consisted of two parts: Catholicism and Protestantism, with Roman Catholicism and Eastern Orthodoxy included under Catholicism. In the last 25 years, almost all Church leaders unanimously recognize that a "third wave" has emerged — a Charismatic, evangelical Christianity which seeks to uphold the book of Acts as the ideal for the Church.

Within this third wave, there is great diversity. Its common denominator is the belief that the Bible is God's Word. According to statistical information from the Lausanne Movement Statistics Task Force, nine out of every ten newly born-again Christians join churches within this third wave.

In the year 1900, 0.7 percent of all those who claimed Christianity as their religion were members of an evangelical or Charismatic church. In 1970, this percentage had grown to 6.2. By 1997, approximately 27.5 percent (some estimates are higher, up to 33 percent) of all Christians belonged to either Charismatic or evangelical churches.

It's harvest time.

SIGN NUMBER THREE:

EVENTS IN SOUTH AMERICA AND AFRICA

At the turn of the century, 3 percent of Africa's population were either actual or nominal Christians. Most of these were found in Egypt and Ethiopia within the Coptic Church, where conversion and the born-again experience are not emphasized. Today, 40 percent of Africa's population claim Christianity as their belief, and approximately three-quarters of these are born-again Christians.

At the turn of the century, South America had virtually no evangelical believers. Current growth trends reported in secular newspapers suggest that South America will be an evangelical continent within a few decades. The Pope has expressed concern and has traveled repeatedly to South America for the purpose of rallying support for the declining Roman Catholic Church. Today South and Central America have more than 75 million evangelical Christians.

It's harvest time.

SIGN NUMBER FOUR:

CHANGES IN THE FORMER COMMUNIST WORLD

For most of my adult life I lived in a world where it was unthinkable to preach the Gospel in countries such as Russia, Estonia, Latvia, Lithuania, Bulgaria, Romania, and Hungary. These and numerous other countries were considered "closed" to the Gospel. In the last few years, hundreds of millions of "communists" who had virtually no previous knowledge of Christ have heard the Gospel.

In our ministry, we have distributed millions of booklets to people in Eastern Europe who have responded to the invitation in our crusades to receive Christ.

Though some countries are still at least partially "closed," such as China, Cuba, and North Korea, reports of revival are beginning to surface out of some of these nations, particularly China. In 1949 there were an estimated one million Catholics and one million Protestants in China. Today, estimates range as high as one hundred million believers inside China.[2]

It's harvest time.

SIGN NUMBER FIVE:

THE POPULATION EXPLOSION

Today the world population is larger than it has ever been. Therefore, in order to win the largest number of souls in human history, the great harvest could come in our generation. Two thousand years ago, approximately 175 million people populated the earth. By 1850 the numbers reached one billion. By 1930 estimates of that number had doubled, and in 1960 three billion people were on the earth.

By 1988 the earth's population exceeded five billion. In 1994 it was 5.6 billion. In the new millennium, the world population will be between six and seven billion. At the current growth rate, the earth's population will reach 14 billion by A.D. 2050. (See graph on page 178.)

The great spiritual harvest which Jesus prophesied will take place at a time when the world's population is at its peak and will, quite conceivably, result in heaven being far more populated than hell.

SIGN NUMBER SIX:

THE RATIO OF BELIEVERS TO NONBELIEVERS

The U.S. Center for World Missions in Pasadena, California, led by Dr. Ralph Winter, publishes some of the best researched world missions statistics available. To understand their findings, one needs to recognize the definitions used in reference to the term "Christian." Dr. Winter speaks of "non-Christians," "nominal Christians," and "Bible-believing Christians."

The term "Bible-believing Christians" refers to those who count themselves as being born again and saved by the blood of Jesus. These are the kind of people who believe that the Bible is a guide for life, and they believe in the need to evangelize the world.

"Nominal Christians" would be those who are "culturally Christian," but do not confess a personal relationship with Jesus Christ.

- By the year A.D. 100, there were 360 non-Christians on the earth for every Bible-believing Christian.

- By the year 1500, there were 69 non-Christians for every Bible-believing Christian.
- By 1900, there were 27 non-Christians for every Bible-believing Christian.
- In 1950 there were 21 non-Christians to every Bible-believing Christian.
- By 1995, there were approximately ten non-Christians for every Bible-believing Christian.

The trend is in the Church's favor. Though we have not yet seen the fullness of the earth's harvest, we are seeing its beginning.

SIGN NUMBER SEVEN:

THE ACCELERATION IN WORLD EVANGELISM

The acceleration in world evangelism which Jesus promised in Luke 14:16-23 can be compared to the following statistics from the Lausanne Movement Statistics Task Force:

- After the first 1400 years of the Church (from approximately A.D. 30 to A.D. 1430) about 1 percent of the earth's population were Bible-believing Christians.
- After an additional 360 years (by 1790) that figure was 2 percent.

- After an additional 150 years (by 1940) the figure reached 3 percent.
- Then, in just 20 years, from 1940 to 1960, another percentage was added, so that in the year 1960, 4 percent of the earth's population were Bible-believing Christians.
- In the next decade came another percentage increase, and the same repeated in the 1970s, so that by 1980, 6 percent of the world's population were Bible-believing Christians.
- In the 1980s, however, things accelerated at a much quicker rate, so that by 1990 it was estimated that 9 percent of the earth's population were Bible-believing Christians.

The Statistics Task Force also claims that 70 percent of all world missions efforts have been made in this century.

Seventy percent of evangelism and missions work in this century has been done after World War II (1945).

And 70 percent of what has happened since 1945 occurred in the three years prior to the 1990 Lausanne report.[3]

Again, the signs point to an enormous acceleration. The harvest of the earth is upon us.

SECTION 4

THE FINAL SIGN

CHAPTER 15

THE FINAL SIGN THAT MUST BE FULFILLED

THE NEW MILLENNIUM HAS GENERATED an abundance of predictions about the return of Jesus. Preachers and teachers everywhere are talking about the signs of His coming. In this book, we have pinpointed the one event, the one and only thing that, with absolute certainty, shows how and when Jesus will come back. The one sign of Christ's coming that must be fulfilled is the completion of the evangelization of the world. "The last trumpet" indicates that the last region of the earth has been reached.

The "harvest" speaks of an outpouring of God's Spirit when the entire world will be touched. Remember the end-time acceleration (Chapter 12)?

The scripture that summarizes all these prophecies is Matthew 24:14:

> **"And this gospel of the kingdom will be preached in all the world as a witness to all the nations, and then the end will come."**

> **The disciples did not ask for *the signs* of His coming...They asked for *the* sign.**

Many sermons have been preached about the signs of the times found in Matthew, chapter 24. To properly understand Jesus' teaching we must note that the disciples did not ask for *the signs* (plural) of the time, but for *a sign* (singular): **"What will be the sign of Your coming, and of the end of the age?"** (Matthew 24:3).

We must assume Jesus answered the question the disciples asked, not the questions they didn't ask. The disciples did not ask for the *signs* of His coming and the end of the age. They asked for *the* sign.

Jesus began His answer to this question by mentioning many coming world events: wars, famines, pestilences, earthquakes, false prophets, and lawlessness. However, He assured His disciples that these were merely **the beginning of sorrows** (v. 8) and that **the end is not yet** (v. 6).

Through all these difficulties, believers were to endure to the end. (v. 13.) It is obvious by the way Jesus used the phrase, "endure to the end" that none of these difficulties were the end or even *the* sign of the end.

On the one hand, Jesus enumerated events and happenings that were general indications the end was approaching.

Then He responded to the actual question of the disciples concerning what would be *the* definite sign of the end.

That definite sign is the preaching of the Gospel of this kingdom as a witness to all ethnic groups. Jesus said, **Then the end will come** (v. 14).

As mentioned in Chapter 2, a casual presentation of the Gospel is not sufficient to fulfill Matthew 24:14. The **gospel of the kingdom** is the Gospel of the rule, authority, and power of Christ. Some of the areas where Christ exercises His authority and rule are seen through changed lives, the healing of the sick, and the building up of local churches. The term "witness of the Gospel of the kingdom" indicates that there must be a visible representation of Christ's rule and power to every ethnic group. "Nations" is the Greek word *ethnos*. All 20,000-plus ethnic groups on the earth must each have the witness of the Gospel of the kingdom of God before Jesus comes back.

The gospel of Mark restates it this way: **"And the gospel must first be preached to all the nations"** (Mark 13:10). Notice the word "first." God's priority is world evangelization.

Will Jesus' return be next year?

Ten years from now?

Tomorrow?

These are the wrong questions. The sign is not a year, nor earthquakes, famine, pestilence, nor the formation of a

United Europe. *The sign* is the completion of the task of preaching the Gospel —

> **"...then the end will come." Matthew 24:14**

In the following chapter I will share facts and statistics. Behind the seemingly cold numbers are real people. I have personally stood face to face with many who have never heard the name of Jesus.

I remember several years ago driving on a major highway going from New Delhi, India, toward the Himalayan mountains. Every few minutes I would ask our driver to stop and, with my interpreter, I would walk into the village nearest the highway. Some of the villages were Moslem, some were Hindu. On each stop I would gather 50 to 100 people. After I had introduced myself through my interpreter, I would simply ask, "Have you ever heard of a person by the name of Jesus?"

Some would raise their hands and answer that Jesus was a schoolteacher, or that someone by that name perhaps lived in a nearby city. On a few occasions someone would say he had heard that Jesus was a religious figure. But the

Some would raise their hands and answer that Jesus was a schoolteacher.

vast majority would shake their heads and openly admit that they had never heard His name.

Such ignorance of the Gospel is almost unbelievable to those of us raised in a western culture, where even the unbeliever knows that Jesus is a person from the Bible and that He is associated with the Christian religion.

I vividly remember an encounter in one particular village. An elderly woman, on her hands and knees, was using a rock to dig a hole into which she intended to put a pole. I knelt down beside the woman to help her dig. This must have been an unusual sight for the villagers, and very soon a crowd of 100 or more had gathered around us. Through my interpreter I told the people that I had not really come to help this woman dig a hole, though I was happy to do so, but that I had come with an urgent message. My message was about Someone Who was able to deal with the sin problem with which every human wrestles. Immediately I had their undivided attention. Then I posed the question:

"How many of you have heard of a person called Jesus?"

I repeated the name Jesus several times to make sure that everybody clearly heard. Not a single hand was raised. I proceeded to preach as I have done so many times, and all those present indicated they wanted to know more about how they could learn to follow this Jesus.

As I walked back to my car, tears streamed down my face. I was thinking, "If this village, located next to a major highway, has never heard, what about the villages one, two, or even four hundred miles to the east, west, north, or south?"

What will it take for our generation to be the one who resounds "the last trumpet"? What will it take for Jesus to come back in our lifetime? How can we participate in the Lord's return?

CHAPTER 16

TEN CHALLENGES BEFORE HIS COMING

AS WE EMBARK ON THE 21ST CENTURY, the challenge to finish the Great Commission is enormous. The trumpet must be sounded in the last regions of the earth, and the spiritual harvest must be escalated so that it penetrates every area. For the interested student, there are many tools of study, some of which are quoted in this book, to help pinpoint where the needs for evangelism are most urgent.

In Chapter 1 of this book we noted the mass hysteria which took place in A.D. 1000 concerning the coming of the Lord. Here we are 1,000 years later and, again, there is a great interest in the return of Jesus. There are obviously many parallels, but there are also many striking differences. Missiologist David B. Barrett addresses this situation under the heading, *"The AD 2000 Megamagnet,"*

> First is the instantaneous speed with which modern communications can spread news, alarm, panic, even hysteria. Second is today's vast agenda of world missions. In AD 999, the Christian multitudes were largely

> concerned with saving their own skins and had no interest in the fate of the world's 202 million unevangelized non-Christians of that time. Today, by contrast, Christians are widely involved in schemes to evangelize the world.[1]

Yes, things are different today compared to 1,000 years ago. Many are ready to respond to the challenges. In this chapter we highlight ten such challenges.

CHALLENGE NUMBER ONE:

BORN-AGAIN BELIEVERS WITHOUT A MISSIONARY VISION

Before tackling world challenges we must consider the great challenge to see the fire of God touch born-again believers and motivate them to take action concerning the Great Commission. The Church, by and large, displays little concern about the completely unevangelized part of the world, accounting for at least 1.1 billion people.

David B. Barrett and Todd M. Johnson report the following statistics for the year 1990:

- 10 billion pieces of Christian literature of all kinds were distributed in 1990. Of these, only 0.1 percent were used to reach those who have never heard the Gospel.
- 3 billion U.S. dollars were spent on Christian radio and television broadcasting in 1990.

Only 0.01 percent were aimed at broadcasting to those who have never heard the Gospel.

- 54 million computers were used by the Church worldwide in 1990. Zero percent were used in the service of reaching those who have never heard the Gospel.
- Only 0.5 percent of all Christian finances were used to reach those who have never heard the Gospel.
- Only 1.1 percent of all missionaries were working among those who have never heard.
- Only 1.2 percent of all foreign missions money was used for the unreached masses.[2]

I recognize the arguments that can be made — that we should maintain our Christian missionary services in countries where missions have already been long established. Some would add that it is not possible to enter some of the unreached areas of the world with conventional missions work because of political restrictions.

In response to these arguments, we should note that in many conventional mission fields a strong national church already exists. It is well prepared to take over the full leadership of its national programs, which will free up missions organizations to focus on the less-reached areas.

Although it is also true that there are political restrictions in certain countries, those restrictions can be circumvented by unconventional methods, such as doing missionary work under the cover of a profession of a teacher, doctor, engineer, etc. On the other hand, there are countries that have a great measure of freedom, yet very little is being done. India, Pakistan, and Bangladesh could be noted as examples.

The Church must recognize that each believer has an individual responsibility for the Great Commission. Before the judgment seat of Christ we will be held accountable by our Chief Commander, Jesus Christ, for what we personally have done in relationship to the Great Commission.

The cause for world missions is not for those who are "specially" called. It is every believer's responsibility. We must be active in one or several of the following areas:

- Praying for the cause of world missions.
- Giving toward the cause of world missions.
- Sending out workers to reach the unreached.
- Being willing to go ourselves to work among the unreached.

For "whoever calls upon the name of the Lord shall be saved."

How then shall they call on Him in whom they have not believed? And how shall they believe in Him of whom they have not heard? And how shall they hear without a preacher?

And how shall they preach unless they are sent? As it is written: "How beautiful are the feet of those who preach the gospel of peace, who bring glad tidings of good things!" Romans 10:13-15

CHALLENGE NUMBER TWO:

CHINA

Since I was a young boy, China has been close to my heart. My grandfather was a missionary in northern China during its pre-communist era. He spoke Chinese fluently and taught it to other missionaries. My mother was born in China.

Every fifth person in the world is Chinese.

It is still difficult to obtain reliable statistics about China. The situation in the former Soviet Union provides a parallel to what is happening in China today.

In the 1970s and 1980s, reports were received from the Soviet Union that a thriving underground church existed. Still, the vast majority of the Soviet people had never heard the Gospel. In the 1970s some were talking as if the Soviet Union was being evangelized by the underground church.

There were many exciting testimonies circulating about the mighty works of God in the U.S.S.R. While there is no doubt of what God was doing through the underground church, the stark reality is that most people had not heard the Gospel. Time and again, as I have traveled across the former Soviet Union, I have questioned people about what their beliefs were 10 or 20 years ago. Almost invariably I have heard reports that agree with my assumption that atheism was completely dominant.

Similarly, today there are many reports about what God is doing in China. There is no question that great things are happening, particularly in the Hunan province. Yet, these great moves of God are limited to rural areas in a few provinces. When China opens up, I think we will find, once again, a people who have been almost completely dominated by atheistic beliefs.

The book *Operation World,*[3] published in 1993, estimated a total of 68.7 million Christians in China, of which 8.7 million were Roman Catholic.

A research center in Hong Kong quoted an unpublished report from China's Statistics Bureau in 1994 that there were 75 million Christians in China, of which 12 million were Roman Catholic.[4]

A news article in *Newsweek* magazine in 1994 set the figure of Christians in China from 50 to 70 million.[5]

In the May 1994 issue of *Charisma* magazine, Dennis Balcomb of Hong Kong reported between 80 to 100 million Christians in China.

The great variance in these figures indicates the uncertainty with which even the "experts" speak of the current situation inside China.

Because Bible-believing Christians belong to the secret underground church and are not able to evangelize freely, it can quite safely be estimated that one billion Chinese have never heard the Gospel.

Further, if there indeed are 80 to 100 million Christians in China, then at least 60 million of them do not have a Bible. The needs are enormous.

CHALLENGE NUMBER THREE:

INDIA

It was estimated that India's population would exceed one billion people by the year 1998. If the population of the greater Indian sub-continent, which includes Bangladesh, Bhutan, Nepal, and Pakistan, were tallied, the one billion mark was passed a number of years ago.

Most born-again Christians in India live in the south and in the tribal state of Nagaland where there are 18 official languages. If tribal languages and dialects are included, the figure is 1,652. The complete Bible is available in 46 languages. Sixty other languages have at least portions of the

Word of God. The number of Christians is set officially at 2.61 percent (1995). Evangelical Christians, meaning those who believe in being born again through a personal relationship with Jesus, amount to nearly 1 percent.

Seventy percent of India's population is dispersed throughout 700,000 villages. Only 65,000 of these villages have a Christian church (Catholic or Protestant).[6]

Although India is a secular state with freedom for all religions, there has been an increasing intolerance from fanatical Hindu political parties, making Christian evangelism more difficult.[7]

Pastors in northern India have indicated that, in their region, approximately one in 10,000 is a born-again Christian. The majority of people living in India have still not heard the Gospel. The trumpet sound of the Good News must be heard.

At the time this book was written, I had just concluded a major crusade in Jawaharlal Nehru Stadium in New Delhi, India. The crowd in the opening service numbered 40,000. Attendance grew, and on the last night, 130,000 people were gathered. It was estimated that less than 10 percent of the people attending were Christians, the other 90 percent were divided among Moslems, Hindus, and Sikhs.

Having conducted 18 major crusades throughout India, both north and south, I could not help but detect a greater spiritual openness than before. On one of the nights of the crusade, the Minister of State for Home Affairs of the Federal Government of India, the Honorable Sir Seryd Razi, a Moslem, spoke for ten minutes, giving a resounding endorsement to our crusade.

Two hundred thousand books for new believers were distributed, and local churches could not accommodate the follow-up services, which had to be held in a stadium.

A new day for preaching the Gospel is dawning in India!

CHALLENGE NUMBER FOUR:

THE MIDDLE EAST

When we think of the Middle East we think of countries like Israel, Lebanon, Egypt, etc. In *Operation World*'s report on the Middle East, 24 countries and territories are included, from Morocco in the west to Iran in the east.

By the second millennium, the Middle East's population is estimated to be 430 million people, with only 0.4 percent evangelical believers.

There are several countries in which the evangelical population is between 0 percent and 0.1 percent, including Algeria, Iran, Iraq, Kuwait, Libya, Mauritania, Morocco, Syria, Tunisia, Turkey, and Yemen. These areas are almost completely Moslem.[8]

CHALLENGE NUMBER FIVE:

THE MOSLEM WORLD

The Moslem world poses a great challenge.

Thirty percent of the world's Moslems live in the Middle East, and the focal point of Islam is the city of Mecca in Saudi Arabia.

As of December 1995, there were a reported 1.1 billion Moslems in the world, with only one full-time Christian worker for every one million.[9]

Islam is spreading very quickly. When the Soviet Union disintegrated, five new nations with a strong Moslem presence were formed: Kazakhstan, Kyrgyzstan, Turkmenistan, Uzbekistan, and Tadjikistan.

Islam has Northern Africa in an iron grip and is spreading southward, especially along the coastal area of East and West Africa.

In our ministry, we have stayed away from southern Africa, where there is a great Christian revival movement, and have focused on the frontline of the battle between Islam and Christianity.

In crusades in Ghana, Tanzania, Nigeria, and the coastal areas of Kenya, we have seen thousands of Moslems respond to the Gospel. It makes a very deep impression on the people, both Christian and Moslem alike, when a Moslem testifies of the healing power of Jesus, and openly declares that he is converting to Christ.

In 1993 I saw another example of the aggressiveness of Islam. The little country of Albania,[10] where Paul preached almost 2,000 years ago, has become known in our century as the most atheistic country in the world. Enver Hoxha, who ruled Albania with an iron fist, pronounced it a completely atheistic state. Things began to change in the early 1990s, and in 1993 we conducted a crusade at a packed stadium in Tirane, Albania's capital.

While in Albania, I took the opportunity to travel to the countryside. As I entered village after village, I was shocked to hear people playing Islamic music on their radios and cassette players. With freedom being only one to two years old, the Moslem culture was already spreading.

In Albania, the battle lines are drawn between Islam and Bible-believing Christians.

In the end, the Gospel of Jesus Christ will win:

> **For the earth will be filled with the knowledge of the glory of the Lord, as the waters cover the sea.**
>
> **Habakkuk 2:14**

(See also Isaiah 11:9.)

CHALLENGE NUMBER SIX:

WESTERN EUROPE

Western Europe is seeing a decrease in church attendance, at an average of 7,000 people per day. In the United

States and Canada there has also been a small decline, though less significant than in Europe.

One recent report indicated that the number of new believers in evangelical churches in the United States has declined 80 percent when comparing the 1990s with the 1970s. Some of the challenging examples from Western Europe are:

- In France 0.3 percent of the population are members of an evangelical church. In comparison, 7.7 percent of the population are Moslem.
- Less than 0.2 percent of Belgium's population are evangelical believers.
- Only 0.2 percent of Spain's 40 million people are evangelical believers. If all who might identify with an evangelical or Pentecostal Charismatic church were included, though not as members, the percentage might go as high as 0.8 percent.[11]

While not all countries in Western Europe are as unevangelized as the three cited above, this area is a needy mission field.

CHALLENGE NUMBER SEVEN:

THE CONTINENT OF ASIA

Based on 1995 statistics, an astounding 3.5 billion people live in Asia. The continent of Africa has ten times as many missionaries per capita as Asia.[12]

With 62 percent of the world's population living there, we must think of Asia when we consider world missions.

CHALLENGE NUMBER EIGHT:

UNREACHED PEOPLE

The U.S. Centre for World Missions in Pasadena, California, has done a great service to the Christian Church worldwide by its focus on unreached people. The driving force behind this organization is Dr. Ralph Winter, who is also the editor of a monthly publication, *Missions Frontiers*. A recent issue listed more than 1,600 ethnic groups, with a combined population of 2,213,468,000, and only 3,793,000 evangelical believers. Here are some examples of the information mentioned in the *Missions Frontiers*' list:

- Among 20 million Algerian Arabs, there are only two known evangelical believers.
- Among 12 million Pathans living in Afghanistan, there are zero known evangelical believers.
- Among 7.8 million Uygur people living in China, there are zero known believers.

- Among 6.6 million Yi people in Central China, there are zero known believers.
- Among the 29 million Sudanese people living in Indonesia, there are only 21,000 evangelical believers.
- Among 47 various ethnic groups in Iran totalling 57 million people, there are zero known evangelical believers.[13]

CHALLENGE NUMBER NINE:

LARGE METROPOLITAN CITIES

Wherever we go in the world — not just the unreached cities of the Middle East, Asia, and Northern Africa — any large metropolitan area presents a unique challenge. So many "ethnic pockets" are hidden within our large metropolitan areas.

In this context, I often think of the Sikh community of British Columbia, Canada. It is not uncommon to see thousands of Sikhs attending my services in India; yet, in British Columbia it is rare to ever see a Sikh attend a Christian church. Every large city has hidden minorities like this.

By the year 1900 there were 300 cities in the world whose population exceeded 100,000. Today there are 3,800 such cities. By the year 2025, 6,800 cities will exceed the 100,000-population mark.

Megacities, those with more than one million in population, have increased from a total of 20 in the year 1900 to 390 today. By the year 2025, it is expected that there will be 650 cities exceeding one million in population.

I could devote an entire book to describe large metropolises and their spiritual challenges. Let's consider only ten of the megacities.

New York City: Although the United States of America is among the most evangelized nations on earth, New York City, a vast metropolis is, to some degree, an unreached area. Among African-Americans and Hispanics, who together make up about 45 percent of New York's seven million-plus population, it is common for youth either to become Moslems or turn to New Age or other eastern religions.

Paris: Paris has a population of 10,660,000, yet many of its suburbs have neither a single established witness for Christ nor an evangelical church.

Beijing: With a population of 10.8 million, Beijing, the capital city of China, like other great cities in that nation, has few believers. Church activities are under heavy government surveillance.

Mexico City: A city of over 20 million people, Mexico City is a challenge! At its present growth rate, the world's largest city will have 32 million inhabitants by the time of the second millennium. More than 1,000 neighborhoods do not have an evangelical witness, and very little has been done to reach the million Central American Indians or the slum dwellers within the city limits.

Dakar: Dakar has a population of almost two million. It is a medley of peoples with only about 15 evangelical groups. Most of its population is Moslem.

Cairo: With its rapid urbanization, Cairo has an unofficial population figure of about 14 million, though the official figure is at 10,120,000. Many of its inhabitants are uprooted peasants living in squalid slums, largely unreached by the Gospel.

Calcutta: This great city has an exploding population of almost 14 million. Many of its areas are unreached, with only a few churches and organizations currently making any attempt to reach it.

Damascus: This capital city of Syria, with a population of 1,850,000, is one of the oldest inhabited cities in the world. Only a few of its Sunni Arab majority have heard the Gospel.

Bangkok: A city of 6,450,000 inhabitants, it has sometimes been referred to as "the sin capital of Asia" because of its high level of immorality. The 109 Protestant congregations have little contact with the poorer areas of the city. The middle and upper classes are also unreached. They are keenly interested in the occult and show little response to the Gospel.

Shanghai: Another huge Chinese city of 13.3 million. Like its counterpart, Beijing, Shanghai is largely unreached. Most of its inhabitants are atheists, Buddhists, or animists.

The vast list of almost untouched cities is endless: Brussels, Madrid, Casablanca, Montreal, Karachi, and hundreds of others.[16]

CHALLENGE NUMBER TEN:

THE PLACE WHERE YOU LIVE

In surveying some of these needy areas where the trumpet sound of the Gospel must be heard, I am sure your heart also yearns for the harvest time promised by Jesus to touch your city, your community, and your family. John's vision on the isle of Patmos should encourage all of us:

> **After these things I looked, and behold, a great multitude which no one could number, of all nations, tribes, peoples, and tongues, standing before the throne and before the Lamb, clothed with white robes, with palm branches in their hands. Revelation 7:9**

Many from your city are in the multitude that cannot be numbered.

THE CHALLENGE BEFORE US

Just before His ascension, Jesus gave His final words to the disciples. This was naturally when He would summarize His most important message to them. He had taught them many things: prayer, healing, relationships, the power of the Word, etc. In His farewell address, He would summarize the purpose of it all.

Each one of the four Gospels records a version of Jesus' final command. Matthew puts it this way:

> **And Jesus came and spoke to them, saying, "All authority has been given to Me in heaven and on earth.**
>
> **"Go therefore and make disciples of all the nations, baptizing them in the name of the Father and of the Son and of the Holy Spirit,**
>
> **"teaching them to observe all things that I have commanded you; and lo, I am with you always, even to the end of the age." Amen. Matthew 28:18-20**

Mark records it this way:

> **And He said to them, "Go into all the world and preach the gospel to every creature.**
>
> **"He who believes and is baptized will be saved; but he who does not believe will be condemned.**
>
> **"And these signs will follow those who believe: In My name they will cast out demons; they will speak with new tongues;**

"they will take up serpents; and if they drink anything deadly, it will by no means hurt them; they will lay hands on the sick, and they will recover."

So then, after the Lord had spoken to them, He was received up into heaven, and sat down at the right hand of God.

And they went out and preached everywhere, the Lord working with them and confirming the word through the accompanying signs. Amen. Mark 16:15-20

Luke expressed it this way:

"And that repentance and remission of sins should be preached in His name to all nations, beginning at Jerusalem.

"And you are witnesses of these things."

Luke 24:47,48

John put it this way:

"As the Father has sent Me, I also send you."

John 20:21

Let us finish fulfilling Jesus' last request to His disciples.

CHAPTER 17

BRING BACK THE KING

JESUS TOLD A PARABLE ABOUT HIMSELF as a nobleman:

Now as they heard these things, He spoke another parable, because He was near Jerusalem and because they thought the kingdom of God would appear immediately.

Therefore He said: "A certain nobleman went into a far country to receive for himself a kingdom and to return.

"So he called ten of his servants, delivered to them ten minas, and said to them, 'Do business till I come.'

"But his citizens hated him, and sent a delegation after him, saying, 'We will not have this man to reign over us.'

"And so it was that when he returned, having received the kingdom, he then commanded these servants, to whom he had given the money, to be called to him, that he might know how much every man had gained by trading." **Luke 19:11-15**

Notice that Jesus told this parable *because* the disciples thought that the kingdom of God would appear immediately. Jesus was redirecting their focus.

Before his departure, the nobleman gave his servants a task to fulfill, saying, **Do business till I come** (v. 13). With the talent each one of them was given, they were to advance the program of the nobleman.

Similarly, King Jesus has gone away from us. Before He left, He promised to send the Holy Spirit to be our Comforter and Helper in the task before us:

> **"Nevertheless I tell you the truth. It is to your advantage that I go away; for if I do not go away, the Helper will not come to you; but if I depart, I will send Him to you."** **John 16:7**

While Jesus is gone, He has asked us to do business for His kingdom in the power of the Holy Spirit. When Jesus comes back, He will hold us accountable for **how much every man [has] gained by trading,** how much gain we have brought to the cause of the Gospel.

Many do not understand or embrace these truths. They have a mentality of church life as maintaining a building, singing songs, having occasional prayer meetings, listening to sermons, and putting some money in an offering plate. God's plan is so much greater! We are the "servants" who are entrusted with a task and empowered by the Holy Spirit

Many have been so preoccupied with...the Rapture...that they have failed to understand that after the Rapture the world will continue.

to engage in world-evangelization business until our Master comes back.

Many have been so preoccupied with their thoughts about the Rapture of the Church that they have failed to understand that after the Rapture the world will continue. God's kingdom will become visible on the earth.

Yes, there will be a Rapture, but after that the Old Testament prophecies tell us of a kingdom of peace that will be established with King Jesus on the throne.

Whenever the disciples questioned Jesus about when His kingdom would come, He always focused their attention on the task He had given them.

The disciples thought the kingdom of God would quickly appear, while Jesus kept emphasizing that they would receive power to be witnesses for Him.

Our purpose on the earth is to prepare the world for the return of the King. I have heard believers say that they live to worship God. While it is very true that we live to worship God, worshiping God involves more than singing songs and raising our hands in praise. If this alone was our mandate, it would be better for us to die and go to heaven where we could sing and play music of praise to the Lord 24 hours a day. (See Revelation 22:5.)

Others claim that their main purpose in life is to be students of the Word of God. Obviously, we cannot overemphasize the importance of studying the Word. My own commitment to God's Word is evidenced in part by the fact that I have started Bible schools in several parts of the world, training hundreds of students for ministry. Yet, if we limit our primary purpose to an increased understanding of the Word of God and theology, it would be better for us to die, because in heaven we will know all things even as we are known. (See 1 Corinthians 13:12.)

However, there is one task that we cannot accomplish in heaven — we cannot evangelize and reach lost humanity. This is why the nobleman, Jesus, has left us on the earth to do Gospel business — to fulfill the task He has given to us.

The human element in bringing about God's purposes for the end time is evident in the apostle Peter's writings:

We are involved, not merely in *looking* for the end-time events to unfold, but in *hastening* them to come to pass.

Looking for and hastening the coming of the day of God.... 2 Peter 3:12

The word **hastening** indicates that we are involved, not merely in *looking* for the end-time events to unfold, but in *hastening* them to come to pass.

How do we *hasten* the day of God?

The obvious answer is that when we accomplish the sign that Jesus said must be fulfilled before His coming — namely, the establishment of a witness of God's kingdom among all the ethnic groups of the earth — that makes us co-laborers with Jesus in bringing to pass His plan for the end time.

I basically see only three requirements for those willing to accept the challenge of the task of the Great Commission:

REQUIREMENT NUMBER ONE:

TAKE RESPONSIBILITY.

If even a small percentage of all born-again believers would take personal responsibility for the evangelization of the world through their prayers, giving, sending, and going, the world could be evangelized in a relatively short time. Pastors and evangelists must preach this truth so that faith and accountability arise in people's hearts. It is only when we are dedicated to the cause of world missions, to the point of seeming fanatical, that we will get the job done. Furthermore, pastors must take responsibility in commissioning workers from their local churches to take the Gospel farther.

The prophet Jonah did not have a proper perspective of others. In chapter 4 of his book, we read how he alternately rejoiced and grieved over a bush, which the Lord caused first to grow and to shade Jonah, and then to be destroyed by a worm devouring its roots.

In His conversation with Jonah, God pointed out that, if Jonah cared for a bush, should He not care for the lost and dying people of Nineveh?

> **"And should I not pity Nineveh, that great city, in which are more than one hundred and twenty thousand persons who cannot discern between their right hand and their left — and much livestock?"**
>
> **Jonah 4:11**

Similarly, we must keep all things in their proper perspective and see the focus of the heart of God for others. When we keep our focus on the commission Jesus gave us, we can expect material blessings:

> **"But seek first the kingdom of God and His righteousness, and all these things shall be added to you."**
>
> **Matthew 6:33**

The fulfillment of the Great Commission is critical. The world is in a spiritual crisis.

In times of crisis, we do the unusual.

For example, we may treasure our new car, not allowing anyone to eat in it for fear they might soil its beautiful upholstery. Yet, if we were traveling along a deserted road and saw a car in the ditch with its driver thrown out the window, bleeding and unconscious, would we not forget about our beautiful upholstery? Would we not put the bleeding person in the backseat of our car and rush him or her to the nearest hospital?

Yes, in times of emergency, we respond in an unusual way. There is an emergency concerning the Great Commission. Heaven is in a hurry. Perishing souls must hear the Gospel.

REQUIREMENT NUMBER TWO:

HAVE A PROPER VIEW OF FINANCES.

In some Charismatic churches, there has been a lot of teaching about the release of finances into God's kingdom. I have personally taught this truth because the Bible clearly tells us that the wealth of the wicked is laid up for the just:

> **But the wealth of the sinner is stored up for the righteous. Proverbs 13:22**

The prophet Haggai wrote of the latter house of God, which is a picture of the Church filled with precious things. (See Haggai 2:9.) To see finances released in a great way, we must go beyond the tithing principle into the stewardship principle, where we understand that everything we have belongs to God. A steward is a manager, not an owner. Once this fact becomes a revelation, we can begin to tap into the harvest principle which Paul taught to the Corinthian church:

> **But this I say: He who sows sparingly will also reap sparingly, and he who sows bountifully will also reap bountifully.** **2 Corinthians 9:6**

In this teaching, Paul attributed harvest potential to finances. We can plant one potato and receive 20 in return, because the potato has harvest potential. In the same manner, our finances, when consecrated to God and sown into His worldwide program, take on harvest potential. It is when we tap into this divine principle that true superabundance is released upon us, individually, and upon our ministries.[1]

REQUIREMENT NUMBER THREE:

PREACH WITH SIGNS AND WONDERS.

It was never God's plan that the Gospel be preached only with intellectual logic and persuasion:

> **And my speech and my preaching were not with persuasive words of human wisdom, but in demonstration of the Spirit and of power,**
>
> **that your faith should not be in the wisdom of men but in the power of God.** **1 Corinthians 2:4,5**

The city of Samaria believed because Philip preached the Gospel with signs and wonders. (See Acts 8.)

The people in Lystra believed when Paul preached the Gospel and healed the crippled man. (See Acts 14:10.)

The people followed Jesus when they saw the miracles He did on the sick. (See John 6:2.)

It is this principle of preaching the Gospel with signs and wonders that has helped me to literally reach millions in mass crusades. In my book *Fire From Heaven* I tell the story of the miracle power of God demonstrated in city after city throughout eastern Europe. Without signs and wonders, healings, and miracles, we may have preached only to a few thousand. But because of supernatural signs, wonders, and miracles, several hundred thousand individuals have been reached at one time.

Are you willing to dedicate yourself to see Matthew 24:14 fulfilled?

Are you willing to see Jesus Christ come back to earth in our lifetime?

Are you willing to be totally dedicated to the task given to us by Jesus?

Are you willing to be like Paul, unashamed of the Gospel of Jesus Christ because it is the power of God?

Are you willing to be used by God to deliver mankind from sin, sickness, and demon powers?

Are you willing to give yourself to prayer?

Are you willing to preach the Gospel in the power of the Holy Spirit?

Are you willing to be a financial steward, one who believes God for money which can be channeled into His kingdom to support world missions among the unreached?

Are you willing to give out of your finances, whether your resources are large or small, for the cause of world missions, meanwhile expecting God's promise of harvest potential to be applied to your finances?

If your answer is yes, get ready for the most exciting life that a human could ever live! Jesus' command to you is,

> **"As the Father has sent Me, I also send you."**
>
> **John 20:21**

Let's see Jesus come back in our generation!

ENDNOTES

CHAPTER 1

[1]David B. Barrett and Todd M. Johnson, *Our Globe and How To Reach It* (Birmingham: New Hope, 1990), p. 130.

CHAPTER 2

[1]James Strong, *Strong's Exhaustive Concordance of the Bible* (Peabody, MA: Hendrickson Publishers), #1484.

[2]Philip Babcock Gove, ed., *Webster's Third New International Dictionary* (Springfield, MA: Merriam-Webster Inc. 1986).

CHAPTER 5

[1]*The Amplified Bible* (Grand Rapids, MI: Zondervan, 1987).

CHAPTER 7

[1]The concept of this chapter is based on Chapter 1 from Oswald J. Smith's, *The Challenge of Missions* (Burlington: Welch Publishing, 1984), and on a play prepared by the author and presented by Word of Life Church, St. Catharines' Youth Group.

CHAPTER 8

[1]Oswald J. Smith, *The Challenge of Missions* (Burlington: Welch Publishing, 1984), p. 37.

[2]The Lausanne Committee for World Evangelization, *World Evangelization,* May 1997.
[3]Oswald J. Smith, p. 36.

CHAPTER 10

[1]James Strong, *Strong's Exhaustive Concordance of the Bible* (Peabody, MA: Hendrickson Publishers), #165.
[2]Ibid., #2889.

CHAPTER 11

[1]Stephen Ozment, *Protestants: The Birth of a Revolution* (New York: Doubleday, 1991), p. 92.

CHAPTER 12

[1]James Strong, *Strong's Exhaustive Concordance of the Bible* (Peabody, MA: Hendrickson Publishers), #2036.
[2]Ibid., #1521.
[3]Ibid., #315.

CHAPTER 14

[1]*Macleans,* "The New Spirituality," October 10, 1994, p. 3.
[2]*Charisma,* May 1994.
[3]All statistics in this chapter are taken from: 1) *World Evangelization,* published by The Lausanne Committee for World Evangelization, May 1997, pp. 16-17; *Status of Global Missions 1997 in Context of 20th and 21st Centuries.*

2) David B. Barrett and Todd M. Johnson, *Our Globe and How to Reach It* (Birmingham: New Hope, 1990). 3) Todd M. Johnson and David B. Barrett, *AD2000 Global Monitor* (Pasadena, CA: William Carey Library).

CHAPTER 16

[1]David B. Barrett and Todd M. Johnson, *Our Globe and How to Reach It* (Birmingham: New Hope, 1990), p. 130.

[2]Statistics vary greatly about the number of unevangelized people on the earth. Some have optimistically put the figure as low as 1.1 billion. Others claim that the figure is still in excess of two billion. These figures were taken from *Our Globe and How to Reach It.*

[3]Patrick Johnstone, *Operation World,* (Grand Rapids, MI: Zondervan Publishing, 1993).

[4]Troens Bevis, Troens Bevis World Evangelization, February 1995, p. 21.

[5]Issue of *Newsweek* unknown.

[6]Troens Bevis, Troens Bevis World Evangelization, January 1995, p. 7, and "Frontier Missions Update," internet website by David Bogosian, U.S. Center for World Missions, Pasadena, California.

[7]Patrick Johnstone, *Operation World,* (Grand Rapids, MI: Zondervan Publishing, 1993), pp. 273-275.

[8]Ibid.

[9]*Dateline,* Arab World Ministries, December 1995.

[10]Albania is referred to as Illyricum in the New Testament.

[11]Patrick Johnstone, *Operation World,* (Grand Rapids, MI: Zondervan Publishing, 1993), pp. 273-275.

[12]*Missions Frontiers,* November/December, 1995.

[13]Ibid.

[14]David B. Barrett and Todd M. Johnson, *Our Globe and How to Reach It* (Birmingham: New Hope, 1990), p. 22.

[15]Ibid.

[16]All statistics on these major cities were taken from *The Economist Pocket Almanac,* 1996.

CHAPTER 17

[1]Further teaching on financial abundance is available by contacting the address at the back.

APPENDIX

WORLD STATISTICS

All information in the following graphs is compiled from the following research materials:

- Patrick Johnstone, *Operation World,* (Grand Rapids, MI: Zondervan Publishing, 1993).
- David B. Barrett and Todd M. Johnson, *Our Globe and How to Reach It* (Birmingham: New Hope, 1990).
- *Missions Frontiers,* November/December, 1995.
- DAWN International Network, Tilehurst, UK.

World Population Growth

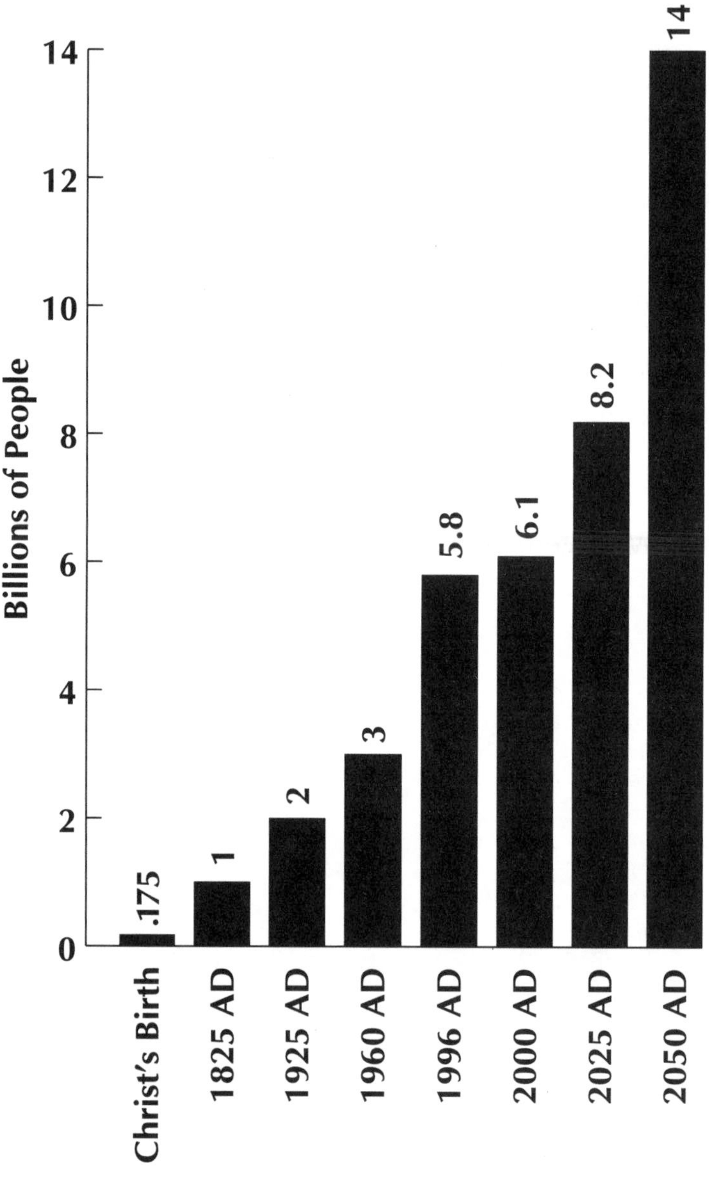

World Metropolises & Mega-Metropolises

Major World Metropolises
(populations over 100,000)

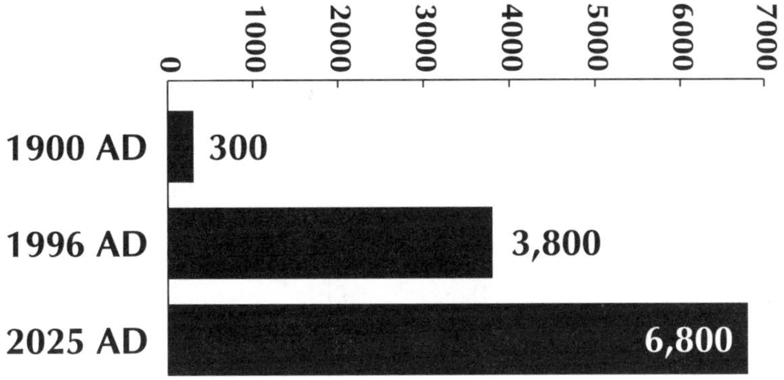

Major World Mega-Metropolises
(populations over 1,000,000)

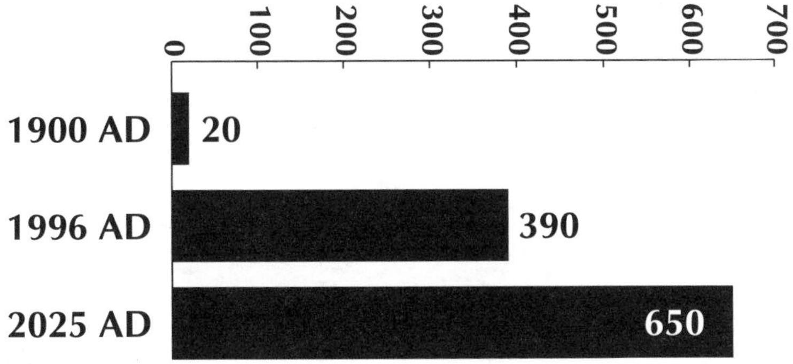

Charismatic/Pentecostal Believers

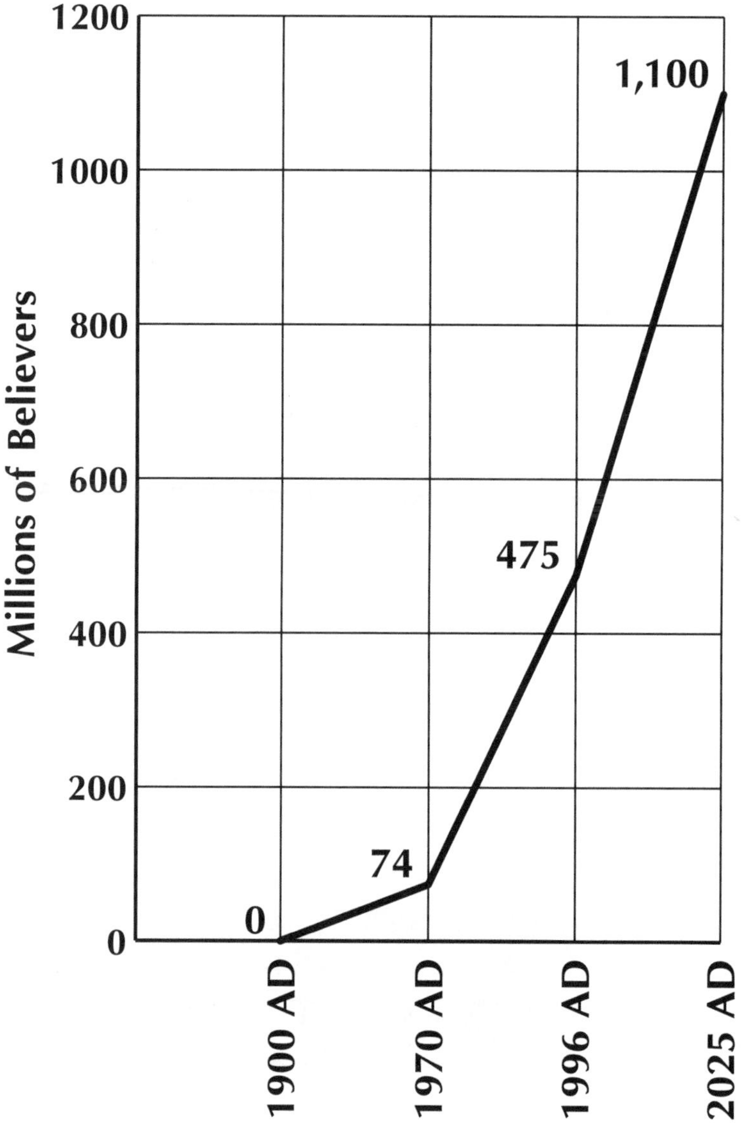

Growth of Bible-Believing Churches

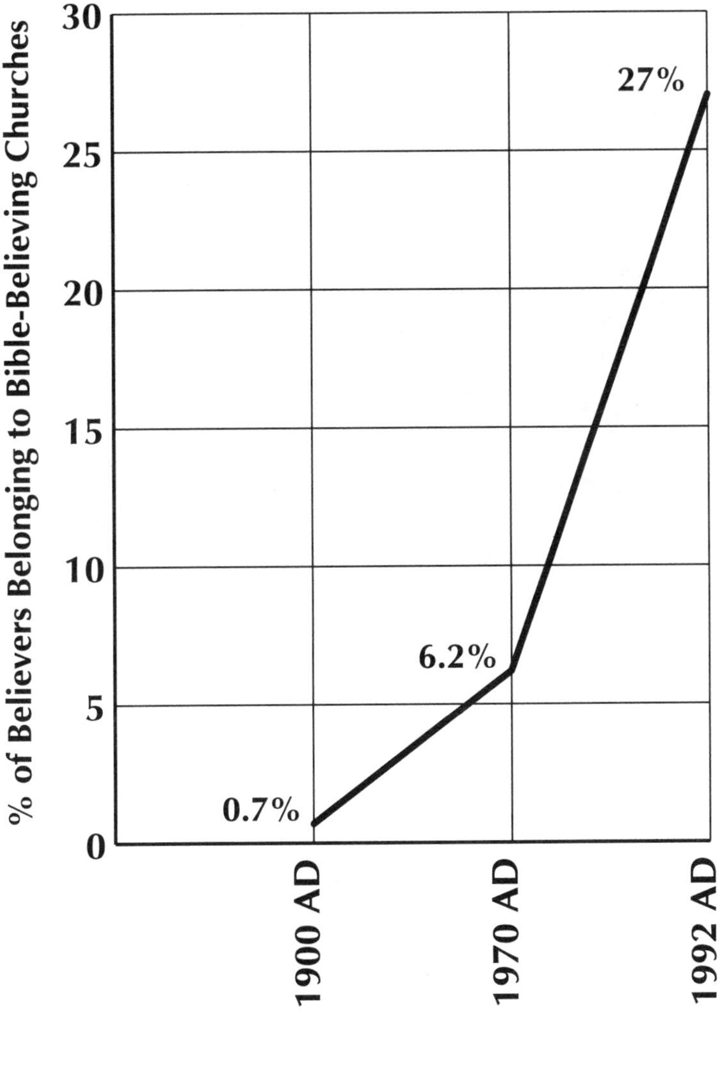

Religions of the World

(±3% Margin of Error)

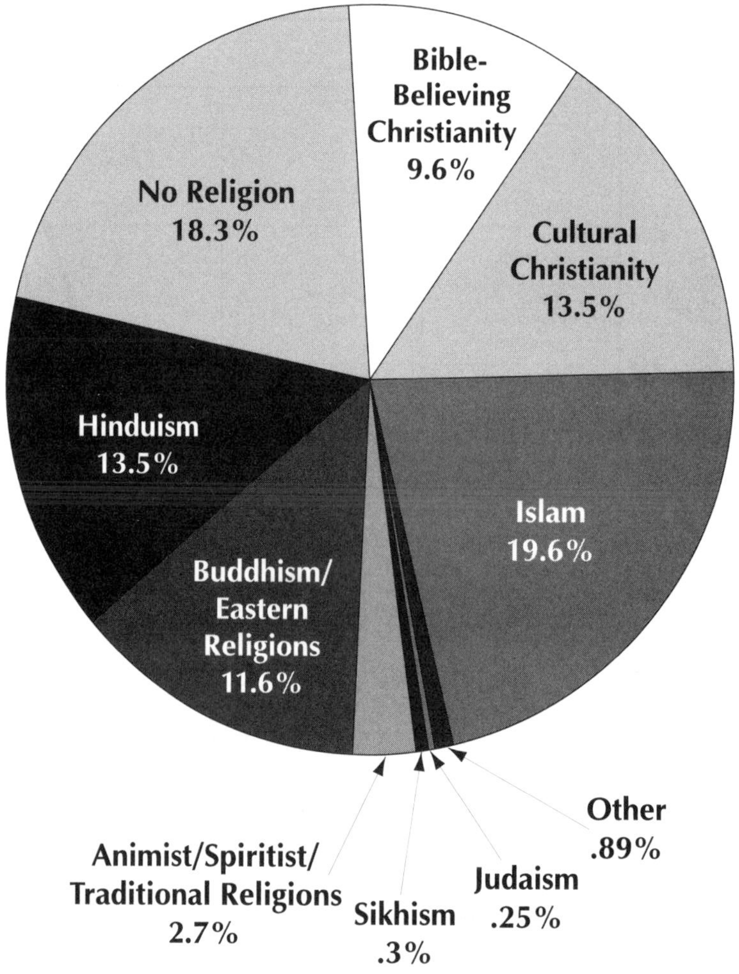

In 1975, Bible-believing Christians represented approximately 3.5% of the earth's population. Today, the figure has reached 9.6% The main growth areas are South America, South Africa, and Central Africa.

Use of Christian Resources Worldwide

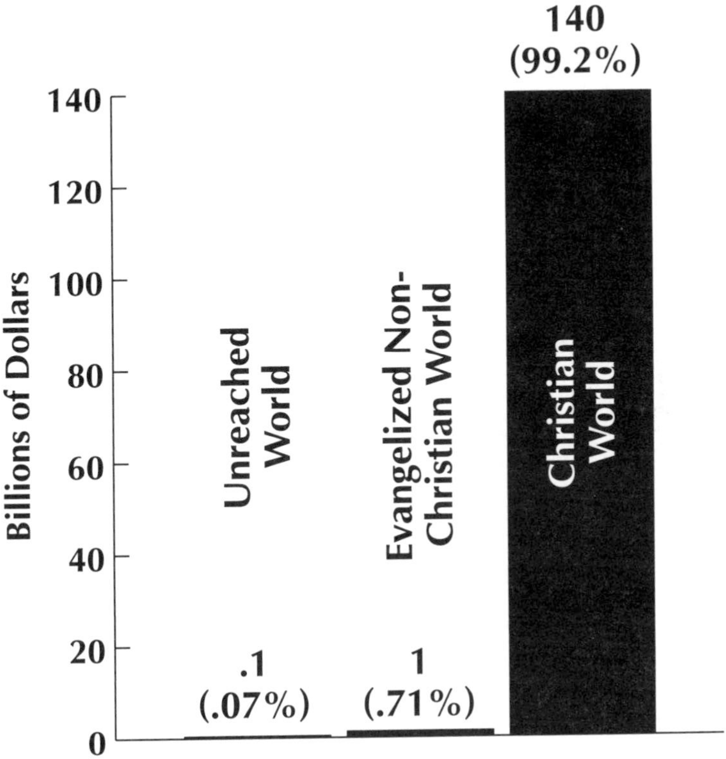

The Unreached World
Those who have never heard the Gospel and who live in regions where there is no Gospel witness.

The Evangelized Non-Christian World
Regions where people may or may not have heard the Gospel, but where opportunities exist to hear it.

The Christian World
Where Christianity (Catholicism, Orthodox, or Protestantism) is the dominant religion.

- 95% of all Christian workers are in the "Christian World."
- 99% of all Christian literature/TV/radio is consumed by and directed to the "Christian World."

ABOUT PETER YOUNGREN

PASSION for the unreached has taken Peter Youngren to more than 100 nations, preaching to crowds of over 300,000. More than 61,000 leaders have attended his pastors' seminars worldwide.

Peter is the founding pastor of Word of Life Church and the president and founder of World Impact Bible Institute, both located in St. Catharines, Ontario. He also hosts a television program entitled, "Global Harvest Force with Peter Youngren," seen on both cable and network television across Canada and in parts of the United States. It also can be seen by satellite in 22 countries throughout Europe.

In 1976 Peter established World Impact Ministries, dedicated to fulfilling the mandate of Matthew 24:14 (KJV) "And this gospel of the kingdom shall be preached in all the world for a witness unto all the nations; and then shall the end come."

His wife RoxAnne shares compassionately in the ministry, and they live in Ontario's Niagara Peninsula with their four children.

For a complete list of materials
available from Peter Youngren, write to:

World Impact Ministries
In USA:
P. O. Box 1891
Niagara Falls, NY 14302

In CANADA:
P. O. Box 968
St. Catharines, ON L2R 6Z4

or call:
1-800-275-2713

Copies of this book are available
from your local bookstore.

ALBURY
PUBLISHING
TULSA, OKLAHOMA

Albury Publishing
P. O. Box 470406
Tulsa, Oklahoma 74147-0406

In Canada, contact:
Word Alive
P. O. Box 570
Niverville, Manitoba
Canada ROA 1EO

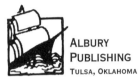